Dear Reader:

The book you are about to read is the latest bestseller from the St. Martin's True Crime Library, the imprint the *New York Times* calls "the leader in true crime!" Each month, we offer you a fascinating account of the latest, most sensational crime that has captured the national attention. St. Martin's is the publisher of bestselling true crime author and crime journalist Kieran Crowley, who explores the dark, deadly links between a prominent Manhattan surgeon and the disappearance of his wife fifteen years earlier in THE SURGEON'S WIFE. Suzy Spencer's BREAKING POINT guides readers through the tortuous twists and turns in the case of Andrea Yates, the Houston mother who drowned her five young children in the family's bathtub. In Edgar Award–nominated DARK DREAMS, legendary FBI profiler Roy Hazelwood and bestselling crime author Stephen G. Michaud shine light on the inner workings of America's most violent and depraved murderers. In the book you now hold, HEARTLESS, acclaimed author Michele R. McPhee takes a closer look at the trial of a man accused of murdering his wife and daughter.

St. Martin's True Crime Library gives you the stories behind the headlines. Our authors take you right to the scene of the crime and into the minds of the most notorious murderers to show you what really makes them tick. St. Martin's True Crime Library paperbacks are better than the most terrifying thriller, because it's all true! The next time you want a crackling good read, make sure it's got the St. Martin's True Crime Library logo on the spine—you'll be up all night!

Charles E. Spicer, Jr.
Executive Editor, St. Martin's True Crime Library

Praise for Michele R. McPhee
and *Heartless*

"Once again, Michele McPhee has gone where others have feared to go. Her writing is as fast-paced as a bullet. And *Heartless* is a must-read for anyone with even a passing interest in true crime."

—Ed Hayes, New York City attorney
and author of *Mouthpiece*

HEARTLESS

The True Story of Neil Entwistle and the Brutal
Murder of His Wife and Child

MICHELE R. McPHEE

St. Martin's Paperbacks

HEARTLESS

Copyright © 2008 by Michele R. McPhee.

Cover photo of house © Reuters / Jessica Rinaldi. Cover photo of Entwistles © REX USA LTD.

ISBN: 0-312-94776-3
EAN: 978-0-312-94776-7

Printed in the United States of America

St. Martin's Paperbacks edition / June 2008

St. Martin's Paperbacks are published by St. Martin's Press, 175 Fifth Avenue, New York, NY 10010.

10 9 8 7 6 5 4 3 2 1

*For all victims of domestic violence
in Massachusetts and across the country*

ACKNOWLEDGMENTS

I WOULD LIKE TO thank Charles Spicer at St. Martin's Press for offering me the chance to break into a house with such a distinguished stable of stalwart true crime writers. Thanks to his co-editors Michael Homler and Allison Caplin.

I have enormous gratitude for my agent, Jane Dystel, who did all the hard work of banging down doors to get this book published, all while remaining unceasingly patient with an attention-span–challenged, full-time tabloid reporter.

Dave Wedge, my former colleague at the *Boston Herald*, did an incredible job helping me find the obvious flaws in this book and researching the stories that formed the criminal backdrop and the political landscape of the Massachusetts justice system at the time of these murders.

This book would not have been possible without the dogged reporting of other *Herald* staffers, including Laurel J. Sweet, Maggie Mulvihill, Tom Mashberg, Joe Dwinell, Lisa Drueke, John Strahinich, and

Joe Sciacca. All of them helped by providing information, or the time to scare some up.

Spiros Motsenigos also offered valuable insight and a willingness to read pages on planes, trains and treadmills when asked.

I must also thank my honorable, distinguished and dear friend Norman Knight for his incessant encouragement.

Finally, special appreciation is offered to my parents, Bruce and Sheila. My godparents, Joan and Dick, are wonderful, as are my sisters, Shannon and Erin. Thanks also to my cousins Chris and Cliff, who are more like brothers, and friends who are extended family, including the Capogreco clan.

And of course I have to recognize Bobby D.

PROLOGUE

THE KICK CAME FAST and brutally hard, dropping Neil Entwistle straight to the prison floor. Entwistle was tall and seemed strong enough, but his back hunched slightly forward, pulled by his paunch. Moreover, though 28, he had an old man's pallor, with skin the grayish color of fading newspaper, the product of too much time spent indoors, inside his rented suburban McMansion, playing video games or eating gourmet ice cream with his wife after they'd put their baby daughter to bed. Certainly, he wasn't a man accustomed to taking a boot delivered with the ferocity and sheer exuberance that only an accused killer who had been diagnosed as a paranoid schizophrenic could muster. In fact, his attacker, Eben Sewall Howard, reminded Entwistle of a football hooligan who seemed to vibrate with a wellspring of rage that could erupt periodically without cause or warning. Soccer never picked up steam in the U.S., but in England, fans can be rabid and dangerous. Thugs traveled in gangs with the sole purpose of sparking mayhem at soccer matches back in his native England.

The assessment was not that far off. By then, Howard had already been charged with attacking an elderly black janitor at a mental institution in Belmont, Massachusetts, seemingly without provocation, screaming, "You raped my mother!" along with a cascade of racist epithets as he wrapped his hands around the old man's throat. "He was obviously delusional," his attorney, Jeffrey Denner, said, and indicated that the case would eventually be pleaded down to assault. Howard was accused of that assault while out on $100,000 bail in connection with another one that had deadly consequences. Prosecutors believe he'd taken a Greyhound bus 775 miles from his home state of Massachusetts to rural North Carolina, where he got into a scuffle with the new boyfriend of his son's mother. That man, Dave Wesley Johnson II, ended up dead, his throat crushed. Howard's handiwork, police believe.

What's ironic, though, is that before Howard started down his violent path, he was exactly the type of man whom Entwistle was obsessed with sidling up to. Howard grew up in Marblehead, Massachusetts— a wealthy oceanfront community on the North Shore that boasted some of the most elaborate and ornate seaside mansions in the entire state. He was the son of a prominent attorney, Richard Howard, who went to extreme lengths to help Eben combat his emerging mental illness. After the 2003 murder charge in North Carolina, the senior Howard hired Boston's most venerable—and expensive—criminal attorney, Jeffrey Denner, to help his son build a defense. Denner managed to wangle a bail package for the strapping blonde 33-year-old and bring him back to Massachusetts. It was the beating of the janitor during his court-ordered psychiatric evaluation at McLean Hospital that landed Howard in the same jail as Entwistle months later. By October of 2007, his attorney was working with North Carolina authorities to make a guilty plea.

But Entwistle had no way of knowing any of that. As far as he was concerned, Howard was just another of the 300 sweaty bodies crammed into a jail built to hold 170 men. He was just another low-life, one of 45 accused killers held there, whose poor hygiene left the entire jail reeking with an overwhelming stench of stale piss and body odor, a stench that caught in Entwistle's throat, practically strangling him. Because of that, there was a vague sense of relief that came with Howard's kick. Entwistle was finally able to cough up the acidy bile that had been collecting in the pit of his stomach as he crumpled to the floor. Perhaps it was the kick from the unknown, faceless inmate that brought Entwistle crashing into his ugly new reality—one not of the suburban bliss of just weeks before, but of case-hardened jailhouse mayhem.

As Entwistle lay sprawled face-down on the cold, dirty linoleum, a pack of corrections officers grappled with Howard, who was now like a frantic human gyroscope, twisting his body around and around to avoid being restrained. One of the deputy sheriffs, Robert McCarthy, snatched Howard's shoulder while another officer grabbed his torso. In one move, they shifted Howard's 170-pound frame straight onto the floor with a thud. He fell face-to-face with Entwistle. In the second that their eyes met, Howard grinned.

Clearly, Entwistle was a long way from his estate tucked away on the edge of the woods in Hopkinton, the quintessence of small-town New England.

If he was capable of critical reflection, Howard would know that the newest entry on his criminal ledger—assault and battery with a dangerous weapon, his shod foot, on a fellow inmate—would this time gain him some very significant jailhouse credibility. It had become a commonplace tactic for Howard, however involuntary and uncontrollable, to rack up additional allegations as he moved through Massachusetts jails. He had already been charged with attacking another inmate during a ride in a prison van, a case that was also among the charges that his attorney was trying to get him out of, his lawyer acknowledged. But getting to Neil Entwistle was a different matter altogether. There was not a single man in the entire prison system who would protect Entwistle from attack. There was no prison gang that would have him; no beefy lover who would protect the effete Brit in exchange for sexual favors. Even the corrections officers might turn a blind eye.

It was true that Neil Entwistle looked immediately weak, and therefore unlikable, with a girlish haircut and soft, small hands. Even his nose, rounded at the end like a designer light bulb, looked like something drawn in a comic. One could tell he took care with his wavy, brown hair. But aside from looking effeminate, Neil Entwistle was accused of a crime that very few people, even those who, themselves, have been accused of unimaginable violence, could wrap their minds around.

Months before, Entwistle, it was said by investigators, had shot his 9-month-old baby daughter, Lillian, in the stomach and then turned the small-caliber gun on his wife, Rachel, and pumped a bullet into her head as the mother and daughter slept curled next to each other in the family bed. The bullet that killed Lillian had passed through her tiny body and hurtled into Rachel's torso. Then, investigators say, he covered his baby's face—bruised blue from some sort of blow, mucus crusted around her broken nose, blood caked around her mouth—with a pillow. Court records would later lay out a scenario that would be reported around the world: Neil Entwistle murdered his family as the mother and daughter slept, then pulled a rumpled white comforter over their bodies. And according to investigators, he then calmly walked out of his rented home, climbed into his wife's white BMW SUV, drove 35 miles to Boston's Logan Airport, and fled the country.

CHAPTER 1

IT IS SAID THAT men look for their mothers when they marry. That certainly seemed true of Neil Entwistle.

His mother, Yvonne, was a moderately attractive homemaker who worked part-time as a school cook so she could be home with Neil and his younger brother, Russell. Fiercely protective, Yvonne was the type of woman whose family life remained in the home. She was not one given to gossiping over the back fence. In fact, it was quite the opposite. Located on a typical country lane in Worksop, a gritty town in the middle of England where many found it difficult to get ahead, the exterior of the Entwistles' house received a fresh coat of paint every spring and had manicured lawns. Everything looked pristine on the outside, leading passersby to believe that all must have been fine on the inside as well. That was exactly the persona that Yvonne Entwistle wanted to present to her neighbors, and it was one that was not a huge jump from the truth, especially in light of her family's surroundings.

A large number of the 40,000 or so people who

make up Worksop's population wander through the workaday town without the momentum of academic drive or career ambition. Government handouts are the norm, as entire generations have learned to survive off "the dole." Alcoholism is common in many households, as is domestic violence and sexual abuse. But none of those problems would come near Yvonne Entwistle's boys. She would not tolerate too many strangers near Neil or Russell, and was often spotted playing with her sons in the family back garden long after they had grown into tall, lanky teenagers. The sight of nearly grown men playing sports with their mum gave nosy neighbors plenty of fodder to discuss over afternoon tea.

Worksop, which is located roughly 150 miles from London and is situated on the northern edge of the fabled Sherwood Forest, was once a flourishing town where men came home dusty from a long day in the coal mines, and their wives nursed calloused fingers from their jobs in ribbon factories. It was once a proud place, a town with streets lined with neat terrace houses, where Sunday meals were served in the front "best room" and always included meat.

But in the 1970s, the mines were depleted of coals—and jobs. The women were out of work a decade later when the ribbon factories first became automated and then moved out of the country altogether, for China. Today, there are just a handful of coal mines. What few blue-collar jobs remain come from a plant that makes Campbell's soup and bouillon cubes. As with any city that has seen its industry collapse, the infusion of poverty that follows unemployment brings all the problems associated with it: teenage pregnancy, prostitution, violence and drug abuse. And as Neil and Russell Entwistle grew up under the watchful eye of Yvonne and their father, Clifford, who still worked the coal mines and functioned as a local Labor politician, an influx of Eastern Europeans moved into the town, leading to overcrowded schools and a burgeoning organized crime problem. The once-tidy terrace houses that made up the town in its glory days are today ramshackle, crumbling and, in many cases, menacing, slums. Worksop is certainly not one of the destinations highlighted on tourist maps of England. Unless one runs into the town's most famous resident, rock star Bruce Dickinson, a vocalist in the internationally acclaimed metal band Iron Maiden, there is not a hell of a lot to do there.

Coming from Worksop was nothing to boast about. And Neil Entwistle seldom did. In fact, he was so ashamed of his rough-as-concrete, Cockney working-class accent that he became quiet, a virtual shut-in. Much like his father, who only emerged from his shell while working as a labor union leader on the Bassetlaw District Council, Neil was reserved when speaking of his upbringing, but the truth was, he had plenty to be proud of. In a school where many of the students can't read or write, Neil Entwistle's name is emblazoned on an "honours plaque" that hangs in the assembly hall of the Valley Comprehensive School in Worksop. To this day, the headmaster points it out to visiting parents and new teachers, exclaiming over and over, "Neil Entwistle got top grades."

Those grades helped earn him admission to the

University of York to pursue a degree in electronic engineering and business—noble professions that would have landed him in a world far outside of the one his father was trapped in.

It was not just financial success that Entwistle's university would offer him. His academic pursuits would also provide the path he needed to meet Rachel Souza.

The couple came together in 1999 in what they would later describe as a fated meeting at a tiny boat-house dubbed Love Lane, part of the University of York campus. Rachel Souza was a pretty and petite college exchange student studying English literature, reading aloud with a clipped New England accent honed on the South Shore of Boston. Despite her five-foot stature, Rachel had long, lithe limbs she'd earned as a track star at Silver Lake Regional High School in the suburb of Kingston. She would run through the crimson cranberry bogs that dotted the area around her home, each time pushing harder and harder to beat her last time. She usually succeeded. In fact, it seemed that she succeeded in nearly everything she did. She was on her high school's honor roll. She was a peer mediator. But it was her athleticism that helped make her an excellent rower. She was so good at the sport, she managed to talk her way onto the men's team of York University's Boat Club.

Neil Entwistle, tall, raven-haired and noticeably shy, was her teammate. Rachel found his reserved nature cute where others saw him as standoffish. She could meet his eyes when he stared toward the ground, which is where his gaze often went out of habit. Their romantic connection was forged on the icy waters of the River Ouse in the hours that they pushed off from Love Lane and rowed for hours, facing one another the entire time. Rachel was a fan of Henry David Thoreau, which made sense given the New England author's penchant for rambling through the woods and rowing along the Concord River not far from her Massachusetts hometown. Like her literary hero, it was clear to all who met her that Rachel aspired "to live deep and suck all the marrow out of life." At first blush, Neil's enthusiasm for rowing and his furrowed, scholarly brow must have reminded her of the type of man Thoreau describes in his writing, one who worked to "elevate his life by conscious endeavor." Their shared enthusiasm for the outdoors, coupled with the serenity that came with repeated oar strokes along the river, helped give their love the perfect launching dock.

Rachel "was my cox, I her stroke!" Neil Entwistle would boast on a British website soon after their meeting. They quickly became a well-known couple on campus, strolling hand in hand across the university's 200-acre landscaped park. Neil, who was nearly a foot taller than his coxswain, would always introduce Rachel as "the woman I'm going to spend my life with," and then smile at her with a devotion that made the tiny brunette the envy of many unattached females.

"The boat club was a bit of a breeding ground for relationships, with romance popping up all over the place," the club's former president Owen Rodd boasted to reporters. "But few lasted as long as theirs."

The couple's lives had been hopelessly intertwined for just over a year when Rachel was pulled back to the States so she could finish her final year at the prestigious College of the Holy Cross in Worcester. But through those final semesters, Rachel's heart remained in England. In 2001, she left her tight-knit family and the life she'd built in Massachusetts to create an entirely new one in a foreign country with Neil. They moved into a small cottage, paying $1,000 a month in rent, and Rachel began teaching English and Drama in September 2002 at St. Augustine's Catholic High School in the rural town of Redditch. Neil worked for QinetiQ, a recently privatized technology company that was a subsidiary of the British military's Research and Development arm. It was a huge laboratory that conducted top-secret military testing on war planes and aircraft carriers, along with defense training. The facilities included anechoic chambers, reverberant rooms and a transmission suite—all of which needed top secret clearance to enter. For some, the company was a controversial one because of its alliance with British government, which gave it access to lucrative contracts. Rachel thought it was the bad press the company got that made Entwistle cagey about what it was he did for the firm.

He went as far as to joke about his job like he was a modern-day James Bond. On one British blog he wrote:

*Making bombs and other stuff for a living—would tell
you more but I'd have to kill you.*

Living together proved what Neil had been saying
since his first date with Rachel. Within months of her
moving to England, he posted another message on the
British website www.friendsreunited.co.uk:

*Getting married to the most amazing woman in the
world this summer: Rachel.*

That day came, on August 10, 2003, with a quaint
ceremony at the Second Parish Church of Plymouth,
in Manomet, Massachusetts. The reception was an af-
fair that even Rachel's hero, Henry David Thoreau,
might have enjoyed, as it was held at the Plimoth
Plantation, a village that was built to reenact what it
was like to live in 1627. Weddings held on its grounds
are elegant, yet simple. The hall had high ceilings and
glistening antique chandeliers. Even in the summer, a
small fire crackled in the old stone hearth. The wedding invitation sent by Rachel's mother and step-
father was printed in ornate script:

*Priscilla and Joseph Matterazzo request the honour of
your presence at the marriage of*

Rachel Elizabeth Souza and Neil Entwistle.

*On Sunday August tenth two-thousand and three at
five o'clock in the evening,*

Second Parish Church of Plymouth,
Manomet, Massachusetts.

Reception to follow the ceremony at
Plimoth Plantation, Gainsborough Hall.

Rachel had never looked happier than she did craning her neck to look into her new husband's eyes as they danced to "Come What May," the romantic song from the movie *Moulin Rouge*. She even mouthed the words as they swayed slowly together . . . "And there's no mountain too high, No river too wide. Sing out this song, I'll be there by your side." It was one of those perfect summer nights in New England. The darkness brought just enough of a chill that partners inevitably pulled closer to one another. Even the loneliest, the most disheartened among the guests, could not help but feel buoyed by love that night, wrapped in the glow of a crackling fire and dimly lit chandeliers as they watched the beginning of what all in attendance surely thought was a match made in heaven.

After the wedding Entwistle's parents, Yvonne and Clifford, posted a note on the couple's website reading:

Hello darlings, the wedding was elegant. Neil
you were the perfect gentleman. Rachel you
were stunning. We are very proud of you both.
We love you from mum and dad . . .

The couple honeymooned on a luxurious Mediterranean cruise, and made sure that everyone could share in their happiness by creating their own website, dubbed www.rachelandneil.org. Just like Yvonne Entwistle, Rachel liked people to know how well her life had turned out. She was married to a handsome Englishman. She was going to live overseas. Life was perfect. And she had the pictures to prove it.

The photographs on the couple's website were like the flowers that Yvonne planted in front of her family home in Worksop: a symbol that all was well, that everything was in control, no matter what the circumstances or surroundings. There was a picture of Rachel and Neil beaming on deck of the cruise ship, their sunburned cheeks framed with the kaleidoscopic oranges, reds and purples of the low sunset behind them. They clutched each other's fingers so hard in one photograph that the knuckles on both their hands were red. The embrace had the look of two people who never wanted to let the other go.

Neil had finally met a woman who not only physically resembled his mum, but seemed just as willing to take care of him. And while some women live for work, and others for love, Rachel seemed to have both as they settled into a life in an area that Brits refer to as the Midlands. As a high school teacher, Rachel quickly earned the respect and the trust of her students in both Drama and English. Catholic schools could often be rigid, but Rachel was anything but. She would chat and joke with the pupils, smiling when they would tease her about her New England accent, and was delighted when they would teach her decidedly British words like "flibbertigibbet."

She was one of those rare people who seemed to

have a joyful energy, with never a cantankerous moment. Many of her fellow teachers attributed that to the love story that she had with her new husband. They didn't see much of Neil, who had some sort of secretive job with a military company, but Rachel simply glowed when she talked about her husband, to the point where the school's principal would later remark, "Her joy was infectious for all of us, staff and students."

The couple couldn't wait to have a family. Less than two years after their fairy-tale wedding, Rachel gave birth to a baby girl more incredibly beautiful than either of them could have prayed for. Lillian Rose Entwistle was born in England on April 9, 2005, at 12:57 a.m., weighing in at exactly 7 pounds. It seemed the baby began smiling within minutes of her birth, a grin that filled her fat little cheeks with air. Her face looked exactly like Rachel's, with eyes that were certain to become as dark as her mother's. She was an irresistibly happy baby and her parents couldn't help but take endless pictures of her—beginning within minutes of Lillian entering the world. A nurse snapped a photo of Neil with his arm draped around Rachel's leg, tiny Lillian between them wrapped in a white blanket. Then there was the picture of Lillian dressed as a skunk for Halloween. Another showed her crawling across the carpet with tiny overalls and a green ribbon in her hair. There was Neil pushing an English baby pram with Lillian inside, and Rachel clutching Lillian to her chest protectively, her own face crinkled into a joyful smile. There was a family photo of the three of them on a picnic and another on a boat, all wearing matching sunglasses, with Lillian snuggled into a pink snowsuit with a pom-pom hat on her head. Another snapshot shows the trio on a grassy green knoll sharing a picnic lunch.

Lillian made the rounds to meet the grandparents back in Worksop, a visit that was of course photographed. Yvonne looked as if she would burst with pride holding her granddaughter as her husband leaned into her shoulder and Neil wrapped his arm protectively behind her back. Rachel was behind the camera. That same afternoon, Rachel snapped Neil with Lillian, his chin rubbing against the back of her soft head. The sight made her exchange smiles with her mother-in-law. All was well in their world.

The pictures were all posted on the "Rachel and Neil" website with messages like:

> *Lillian is now crawling with confidence. She's enjoying three meals a day of her Mummy's home-cooked food and is already eating a variety of finger foods. . . .*
> *We love hearing from you!*

By then, Rachel had already earned the respect of her pupils, who felt comfortable enough with their American teacher that they nicknamed her "Enty;" she in turn lovingly referred to them as "Fraggles," the name coming from the fun-loving Muppets on a long-defunct American television show called *Fraggle Rock*. Her students called her at home for advice on not just their studies, but problems in their young lives. Rachel was a welcoming spirit and had a way of drawing people to her. As a result she had already developed a tight circle of friends, other young mums and teachers.

But Neil still felt isolated, much as he did as a teenager playing with his mother and brother in the back garden. He was filled with a sense of impending doom, and began to pass that foreboding onto his wife. Just months after Lillian was born, he began complaining to Rachel that his hardscrabble upbringing was going to hold them back from any real financial success. He had become convinced that his heavy Worksop accent pegged him as a failure, even to perfect strangers. During one argument with Rachel he ranted, "I am never going to amount to anything here because of my accent. I'm a coal miner's son from a working-class background, and everyone knows it."

Neil's sociolinguistic fear seeped into their marriage. For him, the only solution was getting out of England, he told her, at least for a while. Ultimately, he was hoping the family could have homes in both countries. Returning to the United States was fine with Rachel, especially now that Lillian was in the picture. Rachel wanted her daughter to be raised as an American, surrounded by family on the Massachusetts coastline south of Boston, just as she had been. Already, the phone bills were bloated by ceaseless calls to her mother in Massachusetts, and the cost was getting out of hand. In September 2005 Neil Entwistle told executives at QinetiQ that "domestic problems" were pulling him to the United States. Rachel cried when she said goodbye to her students, many of whom also had tears welling in their eyes as they presented her with a bon voyage bouquet of flowers. With that, the family packed up their lives in England and moved in with Rachel's parents in a spacious home on the edge of a wooded area in Carver, Massachusetts.

When they arrived, Neil would confide in Priscilla Matterazzo, Rachel's mom, over a morning cup of coffee, saying with a hint of self-pity, "Rachel was always more family-oriented than me." It was sitting at his in-laws' kitchen table, far from home, unemployed and desperately scrounging to support his young family that it became increasingly clear to Neil Entwistle that it would be not be easy living across the pond.

CHAPTER 2

RACHEL AND HER MOTHER, Priscilla, were more like girlfriends than mother and daughter. They had grown to depend on each other, especially after Rachel's father, Paul Souza, died when Rachel was just 9 years old. Grieving pulled them all—Rachel, her brother, Jerome, and their mom—into an insular cocoon as a tight family unit.

Being home under her mother's roof, especially with baby Lilly, made that bond even stronger. Rachel was pleased that Priscilla had finally found happiness in another man—a workaday divorced dad named Joseph Matterazzo. Rachel's new step-father was tall, with a solid muscled frame, slicked-back silver hair and a seemingly severe demeanor. The truth was that his strong appearance really belied a gentle manner, a calm that was especially disarming when he was around Lilly. It would become a routine—the proud new grandfather would come straight home from his shop, J. Matterazzo & Son Electric in Plymouth, scrub his hands clean and scoop his granddaughter into his strong arms. One of the more touching photos in the

Entwistle family album shows the bare-chested giant cuddling the baby to his broad body, his eyes closed as if in serene meditation.

Joe Matterazzo was the ultimate guys' guy, and certainly Neil—who by all accounts spent more time with his mother growing up than in the company of other men—was not exactly a match. In fact, Neil was often viewed as effeminate, and some even questioned his sexuality. But Neil tried his best to fit in. Once, he went target-shooting with Joseph Matterazzo, a firearms enthusiast who had collected a cache of antique and rare guns. Neil Entwistle chose a .22-caliber to practice with, a small weapon preferred by women or assassins. Other Matterazzo family members took larger weapons. After a day of firing gun blasts at paper targets, Neil watched Matterazzo return the guns to a lockbox in his master bedroom and place the keys in a set spot on the kitchen countertop.

Matterazzo did not notice Neil's eyes following his every move as he went about the routine of putting away his guns and stashing the keys that locked the arsenal away.

The extended family, which now included a saggy-skinned basset hound named Sally who belonged to Neil and Rachel, spent Christmas of 2005 all together. There is nothing more enchanting about living in New England than the Christmas season. The entire town of Carver was stringed with white lights. Red ribbons wrapped around pine-tree wreaths that hung on the front doors of nearly every home. Shopkeepers in the town steadfastly refused to be swayed by some of the efforts in larger retail stores to stop playing Christmas music as a way to avoid offending people of other religions. Songs that had been banned in some big outfits, like "Silent Night," boomed from the speakers of many store windows. Snow seemed to sparkle in the daylight, and icicles dangling from bare tree limbs formed a natural sculpture garden on the town square. Neil Entwistle thought the winter wonderland was magical. Up until this year, his holidays had been spent in a town decidedly more decrepit than the affluent Massachusetts communities he was now moving through. In Worksop, many folks celebrated Christmas in the bar with a holiday pub quiz.

Lilly was just a few months old, but she was aware that it was a special time. In one family picture, Neil hoisted a beaming Lilly up to the top branches of the family's Christmas tree to place her first ornament. In another, he lay down on the floor with Lillian on his chest. She smiled off to the side, clearly looking at her mother as Rachel snapped a picture of the beatific scene. Rachel posted that picture on their website with the caption "I love my Daddy."

As far as Priscilla and Joseph Matterazzo were concerned, Neil and Rachel and Lillian could stay with them in Carver for the duration. Priscilla loved having her daughter and granddaughter close by. But Neil wanted to move his family into their own home. It was stifling to live with his wife's parents, especially when he was having such a difficult time landing a job. He had gone on more than a few interviews in the months since they'd deplaned from England in September, but none of the computer companies showed any interest in him.

Money never seemed to be an issue. Neil had given his in-laws the impression that he was earning $10,000 a month from the English military to advise them on secretive computer programs—certainly enough money to provide for Rachel and Lillian on his own. If they went out for dinner, Neil would whip out a credit card and palm it into a waitress's hand before anyone could pull out any cash. But cash, it seemed, was something that Neil never had much of. The Entwistles lived on credit. Rachel explained that away by saying that Neil's money was tied up in off-shore accounts. Those complications would make the purchase of a home outright impossible, but the couple had started to look for upscale rentals in the communities around Carver.

Priscilla was a little worried about Neil's story. She had been around enough questionable people to have her guard up slightly, especially after her son-in-law gave her a business card for his own high-tech startup that was actually just a folded piece of paper held together with cellophane tape that read "ENT Embedded New Technologies." Still, Priscilla was old-school Boston, given to respecting other people's privacy. Her son-in-law's finances were none of her business. She tucked the card into her purse and forgot about it. But if she had done any research, she would have discovered that the company's address was listed on Tremont Street in Carver—the location of her very own home. The company's website claimed to provide complex technology services, but Neil was using the Matterazzos' Hewlett-Packard home computer for work, not exactly the streamlined network that most techno geeks would require to provide layered web expertise.

Still, Neil had given his in-laws no reason to worry about his dedication to his family. In fact, quite the opposite. It was clear to the Matterazzos that Rachel had found a man completely devoted to her. Priscilla had noticed that Neil looked at Rachel with the same doting stare the couple's basset hound Sally had when she looked at her owners.

And never did the Entwistles' love for each other seem more evident than at Lilly's christening. Neil had a broad grin stretched across his face as he snapped a picture of Rachel holding their daughter after she was baptized into the Catholic faith at St. Peter's Church in Plymouth by Father Bill MacKenzie. Neil and Rachel both rubbed at red-rimmed eyes as the priest prayed over their daughter, saying, "I baptize thee in the name of the Father, and of the Son, and of the Holy Ghost." Because baptism is one of the seven sacraments of the Catholic faith, Lilly's mother saw the sprinkling of water on their baby's temple as the opening of the door into her spiritual life, a candle lit to guide her way if God were to call the baby into heaven.

It was shortly after the christening that Neil and Rachel announced that they were going to move into a rented estate in nearby Hopkinton. The Matterazzos were secretly disappointed. They took some comfort in knowing that the new house was close enough that the Entwistles could still be part of their daily lives.

The sad day came on January 14, 2006. Neil, Rachel and baby Lillian moved into a quaint four-bedroom

Colonial at 6 Cubs Path that was listed on the market
for $549,000. Neil had managed to coax the owner,
Kim Puig, into giving them a short-term lease for
$2,700 a month, telling her that once his off-shore ac-
counts were moved into the United States in twelve
weeks' time, they could buy the house. The Enwistles
gave the landlord a certified check for $5,400 to pay
first and last months' rent, along with another payment
of $2,700 for January.

For the Entwistles, it was a dream house in an idyllic setting. It was painted the gray color of a New England storm cloud, reminding them of the fog that
shrouded the ship that had taken them to Martha's
Vineyard on a day trip with the baby just a few months
earlier. The 2,432-square-foot estate was on a quiet
cul-de-sac with very little traffic, so when Lillian got
older she could play on the expansive front lawn
without her mother fearing the rush of an oncoming
car. The house was among a cluster of eight brand-
new, high-end homes that was part of a development
built with an eye for techies infiltrating the Boston
suburb. It was a far cry from the ramshackle flats back
in Worksop. The house was stunning inside as well,
with brand-new oak cabinets, ceramic tile floors and a
built-in desk in the kitchen, where Neil could work
alongside his family as Rachel fed Lilly or prepared
meals. There were high cathedral ceilings, a fireplace
and a patio with an eight-person hot tub. Rachel could
not wait until it got warm enough for her to soak in
the hot tub with Neil on a sultry evening, looking up
at the starry night. They did not have any furniture to

fill the house, so Neil went to the upscale Rotmans Furniture store and plunked down more than $3,000 on a living room set, and then bought a crib and a bed at Mattress Discounters for another $3,000—all on credit. They took drives around the town to locate the essentials: supermarket, hardware store, pharmacy.

Hopkinton is the type of sprawling New England suburb that movies like *The Stepford Wives* are set in. The town was chosen in 1924 as the starting line for Boston's famed marathon, bringing runners and visitors flooding into the picturesque setting on Patriots' Day every April after organizers decided Hopkinton was more picturesque than its previous starting point in Ashland.

Hopkinton has roughly 5,000 families living there, and almost all of the couples have at least two children, who swim in built-in pools and ice-skate on a scenic man-made lake. The town's Main Street has twinkling Christmas lights during its Winter Wonderland Festival, and hosts ice cream socials and costume parades in the summer. A white gazebo in the town's center is decorated for each holiday. It's truly a Norman Rockwell setting.

Crime is an anomaly in a place like this. Hopkinton is just 20 miles outside of Boston, which had begun recording an alarming spike in violent crime in 2005, an increase in murder, shootings and mayhem that continues today. Hundreds of people were being wounded by bullets on city streets. Commuters climbing off suburban trains from safe towns like Hopkinton were met by newspaper boxes with headlines chronicling the unrelenting bloodshed day after day, blasting news like: "Gunmen's Bullets Fell Three Brothers"; "Theater District Bloodbath"; "Dad Shot as Bullets Hit Stroller"; "Bullets Fly by School Playground"; and "Cops Beg Parents to Help Stop Chaos." And chaos it was in many of Boston's neighborhoods.

Ordinarily, the most dramatic event for the Hopkinton Police Department was a volatile husband beating on his wife, or a drunk driver plowing into a street sign. Children smashing pumpkins on porches Halloween night was a big deal to the cops, and the jolt of car alarms was not dismissed as backdrop noise, as the sirens usually are in bigger towns or cities. The department's chief, Thomas Irvin, oversaw four sergeants, a couple of detectives and just fourteen patrol cops. Nonetheless, it was an elite and professional bunch. Each was highly trained and all had multi-faceted skills. After all, they have time to undergo the best training in the state. It's not a place with a lot of seedy crimes to squelch, drug dealers to bust. In fact, one of the Hopkinton Police Department's anti-crime initiatives was "crosswalk crackdown"—a ramped-up effort to protect pedestrians from overzealous drivers. Another was a concerted push to make sure Hopkinton residents properly numbered their homes so that police could find their addresses quickly in an emergency.

It was the perfect setting for a seemingly perfect family, which is why Neil and Rachel Entwistle were excited about the idea of raising their young daughter there.

Rachel busied herself with decorating her new dream house. Emptying boxes, unpacking dishes. She had no time for updating her family's website. The last posting she would make, just days after Christmas 2005, read:

> *The three of us are doing well . . . The Baptism was wonderful and Lilly looked perfect . . .*
>   *Love, the happy family.*

CHAPTER 3

ON THE DAY THE movers left, January 16, 2006, Rachel was bone-tired. While usually lambent, Lilly was cranky in her new surroundings and more prone to tears at 9 months old than she was at 9 days. Ordinarily, Rachel could not rest if there were tasks left uncompleted. The house was in chaos. Boxes crowded the floor space. And there was tension in the house because Neil refused to answer any of her questions regarding the state of their finances, causing daily spats.

Just that week, Rachel told her mother, she'd tried to use one of Neil's credit cards, but the account had been frozen. Money problems were the last thing Rachel needed as they settled into the expensive new house. Besides, she was worried about paying the $18,000 that remained outstanding on her student loans. It had already been a long winter. The holidays, coupled with Lilly's christening and then the move just months after leaving England, zapped any energy Rachel had left. It was early, but Rachel was going to bed.

Neil stayed downstairs using the family's Toshiba

laptop, which he had procured on credit. He listened until the bedtime noises of running water, tooth-brushing and the pad of footsteps overhead stopped. Then he called up an Internet search engine and typed in a series of troubling words that court documents would later reveal: "how to kill yourself," "suicide," "how to kill someone with a knife," "euthanasia."

The answers to his searches were gruesome. One site describing ways to murder cautioned that

> *stabbing someone to death can take longer than you might think, unless you have the person incapacitated and immediately go for a kill shot. Blood loss that results from striking less lethal zones causes a slower death, and weakens your victim at the same time.*

A disturbing site called satanservice.com justified suicide, saying:

> *The Church of Euthanasia opposes suffering, even for humans. Therefore a Church-approved method must be at least painless, if not outright enjoyable.*

Then he typed in the word "euthanasia" to see the definition of the word. Certainly, he knew who Satan was.

Then he began looking for sex, starting the search at "Adult FriendFinder," where he told the Boston-area users:

*I am in a current relationship, but looking for a
bit more fun in the bedroom and a very discreet
relationship just for fun.*

He even posted a full-length picture of himself,
leaning back in a lawn chair planted in the grass, perhaps a photo taken in the back yard of his in-laws'
home, his hands gripping his genitals. His penis was
fully aroused. One woman he "smiled" at on the
site—sending her an online wink of sorts—was
unimpressed, and turned him down. He exchanged a
few lascivious emails with another woman online,
then shut off his computer and climbed into bed.
Rachel was sleeping deeply, and may not have stirred
at Neil's body weight as he climbed onto their new
mattress next to her. Perhaps he looked over, contemplated waking her for sex, decided against it, and
rolled over on his side, staring at the wall until he fell
asleep.

The next day brought more unpacking, and more exhaustion for Rachel. Lilly was still testy, and crying.
Rachel was looking forward to Saturday night, when
her friend from college, Joanna Gately, and her sister
Maureen were coming to dinner. Joanna and Rachel
had graduated from Holy Cross together in 2001, and
Rachel wanted things at the house to be somewhat
situated for the visit. Joanna was a perfectionist, like
Rachel, so it was important that the dishes be unpacked
and the baby be well-rested. In reality, the place was
still a wreck. Even the new furniture was askew because Rachel could not decide where she wanted every-

thing to go, and Neil was no help at all. But she was too tired to do anything that night. *Tomorrow*, she thought, as she went to bed early for the second night in a row.

As Rachel slept, Neil slapped open his laptop and repeated the macabre Internet search from the night before, typing in words like "murder," "suicide by knife," and "killing someone."

That search went on for more than an hour. Then Neil began trolling the Web for "escort services," adding the terms "Boston" and "Worcester." What came up first was the Eros Guide to Boston, which provided a list of women for every man's preference: blonde, brunette, redhead—and even categories of fetish like transvestites, "shemales," and bondage mistresses. There were others too, like "Eye Candy Entertainment," "Exotic Express" and "Sweet Temptations." But the one that caught Neil's eye was "Blonde Beauties Escort Svc." That site came with a Yahoo map of its location in Worcester, Massachusetts, a blue-collar city just 28 miles from Hopkinton. He could be there in about a half-hour. Then he contacted some of the escort services that he had searched the night before, and printed out some maps.

It remains unclear to this day how Neil Entwistle spent the day's end on January 17, 2005. His whereabouts on that night, and into the following morning, would soon become a matter of great interest. But his wife, Rachel, was sleeping soundly with no suspicion that anything was awry.

The next morning, Rachel asked Neil, gently, about the job hunt. Had he made any progress? Even though she had no reason to worry, Rachel was intuitive enough to know something was awry. After all, she had dealt with troubled teenagers as a schoolteacher. She had grown accustomed to reading people, and there was no question that her husband had begun acting very strangely.

He snapped at her and told her about the interview he had scheduled for the next afternoon at a nearby electronic design company. The state's technology belt was not far from their new home, so Neil had no doubt that he would find a job. He was sure that the money the British government had been depositing into his off-shore accounts would be freed up soon. After all, ten grand a month was nothing to scoff at. The flow was just a little tied up, he assured her. Secretly, Neil was starting to panic. The credit cards were being invalidated one by one. His nerves were frayed. And Rachel had no idea how much trouble they were really in. He was able to whip out a credit card every time they had dinner with her family, and he'd landed the house, essentially on credit, so the fact that they were broke was his own secret shame. He wanted it to stay that way too. Rachel's mother had been treating him like a son. His own parents, aloof at best, had never shown him the same level of affection—they too had been raised to believe that love came with discipline, not displays of devotion. There was no way he was going to let his lies topple him. He had come much too far for that.

This was America, the country where pornographers became billionaires, and technology experts, like himself, were pulling in seven figures with jobs all over Silicone Valley. Neil bought into the hype of all that, and had begun to invest in get-rich schemes that advertised on the Internet. He'd bought into one scam called $$ HUGE MILLIONARE MONEYMAKER, but had failed to make any money. And the roughly $10,000 he had collected running his own spam scams was long gone.

Neil's own schemes had started back in 2002 when he and Rachel were still living in the United Kingdom. He targeted people like himself, looking to make easy money with very little work. One of his promises lured people to send him "just two thousand [English] pounds" that would buy them a start-up kit that assisted subscribers in creating an online porno empire with racy websites that could earn upwards of two million pounds a year. He called his scam MillionMaker and spammed it across the world with the subject line "Make Serious Money—Make Serious Money—Make Serious Money":

> *With MillionMaker you can be sure your investment will pay off, and best of all, there's no waiting years for your return on investment (ROI). We will show you, step-by step, how to successfully promote your adult internet business and generate at least $6000 per month, within the first six months. . . .*

By 2004, Entwistle had moved on to hard-core porno sites of his own: www.deephotsex.com and www.bigpenismanual.com. The sites were registered under the name "Mark Smith," but a search of the URLs came back to Neil Entwistle. The first website boasted paid access to online videos of "barely legal" teen girls performing sex acts, some on each other, and many of them in fetish categories like spanking and bondage.

The Big Penis Manual touted methods to increase the length and vitality of erections, with promises like:

for years we have published information in the field of natural penis enlargement. We have helped over 50,000 men enhance their penis by increasing the overall length and width by up to three inches. These incredible techniques have been used by many people that do not believe in drugs, pumps, or expensive surgery. You owe it to yourself to sign up today and take advantage of our fantastic program.

There were enough desperate men around so Neil could make money off these promises from March until December 2003.

It was then, just before Christmas, that Neil created a website that would bring swingers together. That spam had the subject line "Free Sex = Free Sex = Free Sex." And there was the promise that anyone could make a bundle off debauchery:

We are setting up a Discrete UK Sex Contacts network. To get the service up and running we are offering completely free membership to all who are interested.

He also ran a scheme selling pirated copies of spamming computer software programs that could turn anyone into a successful Internet scammer like himself, luring customers in with an appeal to their greed:

> *How would it feel to sit down at your PC and know without any doubt that you had the ability to make money online? Wouldn't it feel great? You bet it would!*

That scam was registered in his name using the company title S.R.Publications—which had many products to make someone rich, according to Neil Entwistle:

> *We specialise in a varied range of electronic publications, from Internet Business Manuals to our flagship product, the Big Penis Manual. Our range of Business CD's and E-books have been compiled based on independent reviews. While we can not guarantee to make you your first million by the end of the month, the resources here will provide enough information to allow you to be in full control of your finances and earnings.*

But it was Neil Entwistle's own finances that were out of control.

Starting on January 6, 2006, complaints about his products were showing up all over the Web. One eBay executive called Entwistle a model seller since 2004, but admitted that "all of a sudden . . . it went south." The trading giant was forced to freeze the Entwistles' account on January 9, after more than a dozen complaints were filed about him. One woman calling herself Anne posted this remark on a site specifically notifying the public about scams:

> *SRPublications activity stepped up massively over the holidays and a really large scam has been organised that has earnt [sic] SRPublications thousands of pounds in a couple of weeks. It was a very well run and well timed scam, using the holidays to buy extra time, and I think was planned in advance.*
>
> *Some of the software was being sold under the name Neil Entwistle, some under the name Rachel—whether that means both were involved or whether only one, I don't know . . .*

But Rachel didn't know—not entirely. She believed in Neil, but more important, she believed in the life that she had built for herself. Handsome husband. Sprawling suburban home. Gorgeous baby girl. Even if there was suspicion gnawing at her insides, she was willing to ignore it to maintain her image of her complete, albeit parvenu, life. Over the holidays and in the first three weeks of January, when the couple's email account began to fill with angry customers demanding their cash back, Rachel ignored them—even the posting that read "Rachel Entwistle is a bitch." It seemed that Neil had desperately tried to launch copycat sex sites that had earned him some money in England, and sometimes used Rachel's name to register them. All of his get-rich-quick attempts had one thing in common—they all made ludicrous promises, claims that Entwistle himself had fallen for:

> *I can show you how to Make REAL Money with Paid to read e-mail programs! <u>Not pennies per month but DOLLARS per day!</u>*
>
> *You will learn, absolutely FREE, how to multiply your paid to read e-mail earnings so that you will get a paycheck EVERY month from ALL of your paid to read programs. . . .*
>
> *It didn't take ANY money to get it started—just some time on a computer hooked up to the Internet. My juices were flowing now! I had discovered THE magic bullet . . . THE free business..... THE income opportunity.*

Neil's juices may have been flowing, but the cash was not. He talked real big, but couldn't deliver. The Entwistles were flat broke and had accumulated mounting debt. Anxiety was a constant in Neil's stomach. Some people turn to alcohol or drugs to assuage that sense of panic, of impending doom. Neil had developed different addictions: deception and deviant sex.

He had built himself into a prison of lies, and the piles of untruths had trapped him in a life he could not afford. Like any good addict, Neil needed to stuff the feelings he was having with something, anything. At that very moment, on the night of January 18, 2006, the only thing he had to dull the pain, the panic, was sexual release. So he went online, and judging from what investigators would later find on his computer, he stared at pictures of naked women. Given the kind of man that Neil Entwistle later turned out to be, it is very likely that he then pleasured himself until he was numb.

CHAPTER 4

WHERE THE HELL IS she? That's what was running through Priscilla Matterazzo's mind on Friday, January 20, 2006, as she power-called her daughter and there was no answer. Not in the morning. Not later in the afternoon. Not even that evening. She hit REDIAL more than a dozen times, but could not get through to Rachel at home or on her cell. Neil was not picking up his cell phone either. Maybe Rachel was out shopping for food or table linens or last-minute items for the following night's dinner party with her old college friend. But it was unlike her not to check in for an entire day, and Priscilla Matterazzo was beginning to worry.

She had talked to Rachel on Thursday night, an abrupt call, but a call nonetheless. They'd set up a brunch meeting for Saturday so that Priscilla could see the baby, and help her daughter unpack. As Priscilla worried the following day, she had no way of knowing that her son-in-law had spent the hours after her last phone call to her daughter driving Rachel's car to the Solomon Pond Mall in nearby Marlborough. There, he popped into the Yankee Candle Company, a New

England institution for overpriced candles in an assortment of fragrances, and bought four large scented pillars. He put the eighty-eight dollar purchase on his credit card.

The candle store's clerk, Kristin Richard, had no idea how mysterious that purchase would become to police until days later.

CHAPTER 5

JOANNA GATELY WAS IMPRESSED as she drove up to the pretty white house at 6 Cubs Path in Hopkinton with her younger sister, Maureen. *Rachel's done all right for herself*, she thought. The large Colonial was crusted with snow, and glistened even in the dim light of dusk. All of the lights were on inside, so the Gatelys could see the mish-mash of expensive new furniture scattered without design in the living room. The table was set with dishes. Clearly the Entwistles were expecting them, even though the Gately sisters were two hours late for the planned five o'clock dinner.

Joanna had tried to call to tell them about the delay, but did not get an answer. So here they were, standing on the front stoop ringing a doorbell in the freezing chill of a winter night with no response. Frustrated, Joanna began knocking loudly. Then she called Rachel's cell phone. She heard the phone ring inside the house. No one goes anywhere without their cell phone, and clearly Rachel had left hers at home. She had to be there.

Joanna knocked again. No answer.

Strange, Joanna thought. *Rachel is so responsible, she would never have a friend make the long trek along the Massachusetts Turnpike from Cambridge only to forget that they had plans.* Rachel was not the type to pull out at the last minute—especially without calling. After about thirty minutes standing at the door, anxiety began to shorten Joanna's breath. Instinctively, she knew something was wrong.

That sense of discomfort was only intensified when she saw the note that Rachel's mom had left in the mailbox:

Where are you??? Call me.
  Mom.

Gately looked at her sister and then pulled her cell phone out of her purse.

"Priscilla? It's Joanna. I'm here and Rachel and the baby are not. I saw your note."

"I haven't been able to reach them for two days," Matterazzo answered. "I can't believe she wouldn't be there for dinner. She was looking forward to it all week. She talked about it all the time."

Both women agreed it was completely out of character for Rachel not to return phone calls, but more important, she never would have canceled plans without telling one of them. And the fact that Rachel's cell phone was still on the kitchen counter made them uneasy. If something had happened, God forbid, it would have been difficult for Rachel to reach anyone for help.

Just before 8:30 p.m., Gately drove to the Hopkinton

police station with some trepidation. She knew full well it was likely the cops would dismiss her entirely, knowing it sounded ridiculous that she was reporting an entire family going missing—all because of broken dinner plans. She took a deep breath and blurted to the desk officer, "I'd like to make a missing persons report."

It was a slow night in Hopkinton, and Joanna Gately was not subjected to the eye-roll behind her back that cops in other police departments might have engaged in. Clearly, a similar complaint that an affluent young couple was "missing" made at a busier police station, especially in Boston, would have been ignored for at least twenty-four hours, if not entirely. But carbon monoxide deaths are not uncommon in the frigid temperatures, and the odorless, deadly gas could have seeped into the young couple's new and unfamiliar home. Just five months before, seven people in nearby Duxbury were overcome by carbon monoxide and nearly died before being rushed to the hospital. All survived, but the incident was on the minds of police officers in every town.

Hopkinton police dispatcher Sergeant Charles Wallace, a twenty-one-year veteran of the Hopkinton P.D., transmitted a call to the patrol car officers, Sergeant Michael Sutton and Officer Aaron O'Neil, asking them to report to 6 Cubs Path to conduct what police call a "well-being check." Joanna Gately had not been the only one to ask. By the time she turned up at the police station, Priscilla Matterazzo had already called and spoken to Sergeant Wallace, expressing her concerns about her daughter. That call, made at 8:25 p.m., minutes after Priscilla Matterazzo had hung up with Joanna, recounted her visit to 6 Cubs Path for the planned brunch and not finding her daughter's family home.

"I was there today. I can't reach her. It's completely uncharacteristic," Matterazzo told the police dispatcher. "The last time I spoke to her was on Thursday night. Everything was fine then.

"She's not the type to not call in two days. We're in pretty constant contact with each other. And it's totally unusual for her not to be home for her friends. If her plans changed, she would have let me know about it.

"She's the type of girl who calls me every single day."

Wallace tried to assuage the worried mom's fears, telling her, "We're sending someone right over there. We'll give you a call back to make sure everything's all right." The Gatelys returned to 6 Cubs Path to meet the responding officers.

They got there first and met Sutton and O'Neil as they pulled into the Entwistles' driveway. Both cops walked the perimeter of the house and found all the windows and doors locked tight. "There were various lights on. A TV was on in the living room, a dog was barking in a family room in the front of the house," Sutton would later recall. It looked as if the home were occupied.

Sutton—a striking man with short-cropped black hair highlighted gray—pulled a laminated Blockbuster video store membership card out of his wallet and jimmied it back and forth in the bottom lock of the front door. After a few minutes, he heard a *snap* and then pushed the door open. The officers walked into a foyer, then into the kitchen and dining room. In a room off the kitchen they found the source of the barks, a basset hound in a crate.

"Hello? Hello?" Sutton and O'Neil called.

"It appeared no one was there," Sutton said later.

O'Neil searched the basement as Sutton climbed the stairs to the second floor. He heard the soothing sounds of classical music coming from a radio in what was clearly a baby girl's room. But the infant depicted in photographs all over the house was not in her crib—or anywhere else that they could see.

There was no sign of a break-in, and all the windows and doors in the house, including the garage, were secured. Sutton did take note that the table was laid out "as if the family was getting ready for a meal," and that there were dirty dishes piled in the sink. Water filled an upstairs bathtub, as if someone had been getting ready to give the baby a bath, but was pulled away unexpectedly. Both cops climbed the stairs, and noticed that the bedclothes in the master bedroom were in disarray, as if the bed had been slept in but remained unmade. O'Neil would later note, "there appeared to be no one in the room."

Gately had told them that the Entwistles only had one car—a white BMW sport-utility vehicle. There was no vehicle in the garage, the cops noted.

O'Neil spotted a digital camera on the kitchen table and turned it on, flipping through the photographs to see when the last picture was dated. The most recent photo, taken two days earlier on January 19, 2006—the same day Rachel last spoke to her mother—showed a beaming baby girl. Meanwhile Sutton's eyes went to a pile of mail on the kitchen counter, with an open bill on top. It was from the company that leased the white BMW SUV to Rachel Entwistle for $498 a month. Sutton opened it, scrawled down the BMW's VIN—Vehicle Identification Number—and called Wallace, the Hopkinton police dispatcher, looking for the license plate number.

Less than five minutes later, Sutton's police radio crackled as Wallace read off the registration: "six-five-K-Kerry-W-Walter-seven-nine." Sutton ran the plate number through his cruiser's Registry of Motor Vehicles system to make sure that no one had run a "BOLO"—Police parlance for "Be on the Lookout"—or found it abandoned. There had been no queries about that registration from other police departments. And, gratefully, there was no report of a crash involving the vehicle.

Seemingly, the Entwistles had left for the night and not told their friends that dinner was off. Sutton made sure everything was secure inside and walked out to meet the Gatelys.

"It looks like everything is okay here. There does not appear to be a case of carbon monoxide poisoning. It's all good news at this point," Sutton told them. "Can we do anything else for you?"

Joanna Gately was on her cell phone talking to Priscilla Matterazzo. She handed the phone to Sutton so he could tell the worried mother what he had found.

Matterazzo, who by then had begun to cry, asked if there was anything else that the police *could* do.

"Well, we can put out a general broadcast communication with a description of your daughter's car and license plate, and ask any police departments who spot the vehicle to call the Hopkinton police."

Sutton then assured her that he had run the license plate, and the car had not been stopped or involved in an accident.

"Do you have the numbers to all the area hospitals?" Sutton asked the mom.

He rattled off several phone numbers to nearby emergency rooms from a list that he kept inside his ticket book.

Joanna Gately continued to hear Sally barking inside, and remarked that that was why she was so worried. "They never go anywhere without Sally. She's completely pampered. She's a very pampered dog," she told Sutton.

Sutton allowed her to take the basset hound for a short walk and then put the dog back in her cage. He checked again to see that everything was locked securely and pulled the door shut for the last time that night.

"If you hear anything, let us know, because we are going to continue to look for them," Sutton told the Gatelys.

But before he and O'Neil left, he called his dispatcher from the police radio again and said he would be phoning the Framingham and Milford hospitals first so if there were, God forbid, an emergency, officers could be there to help the family. Back at the stationhouse, Sutton began filling out paperwork about the well-being check. O'Neil went home, thinking about the image of the baby girl captured in the strangers' camera.

Joanna and Maureen Gately parked their car in front of the Entwistles' house and settled in. They were not leaving until they knew the family was safe.

It was going to be a very, very long night.

CHAPTER 6

JUST AFTER 5 P.M. ON Sunday, January 22, 2006, Sergeant Sutton looked up from his desk at the Hopkinton Police Department and saw Joanna Gately walk into the stationhouse. She looked pale and disheveled and was flanked by an older couple he correctly assumed were the mother he had spoken to the night before and her husband.

Earlier that day, Joseph Matterazzo had called his old neighbor and close friend Joe Flaherty, who had been a legendary investigator with the state police. Flaherty's specialty had been homicide. He'd led a team of state police detectives who were assigned to the Suffolk County District Attorney's Office, the busiest prosecutorial outfit in the state, into an astonishing 100 percent clearance rate in murder case closures. He was a stickler for victims' rights and was obsessed with bringing justice to the families who had seen a loved one slain. Flaherty had retired just a couple of years earlier, but his name alone commanded a certain level of respect from his former law enforcement compatriots. Flaherty had not seen Joe

Matterazzo in a few years, but heard enough of an edge in his friend's voice to keep the catching-up small talk to a minimum so they could cut straight to the point.

"Joe, I need your help," Matterazzo said in an easy and steady voice. He was so calm, and chose each word so deliberately, it was clear that he was working very hard to keep his cool. "My step-daughter Rachel and her family are missing. My wife is worried sick. They moved into this new house in Hopkinton just about a week ago, and we haven't been able to reach her since Thursday night. It's not like her. She and her husband were living with us all summer. She and her mother are real tight. This is totally out of the ordinary.

"I'm on my way up to their house. Can you meet me there?"

Matterazzo made the call to Flaherty after his wife told him that Hopkinton police had said there would not be a detective available to really dive into a missing persons case until Monday afternoon. But now it was Sunday. Priscilla had last spoken to her daughter on Thursday night. There was an increased sense of urgency that something was awry with the Entwistles, and their family could not have waited another twenty-four hours for the Hopkinton police to help them make sure everything was okay.

Flaherty had been a cop long enough to know that anything is possible. Anything. Robbers could have broken in and left the family for dead. Neil could have had a fight with his wife, killed her, and taken off for his native England with the baby. Carbon monoxide poisoning could have wiped them all out in their sleep. Their car could have flown off some sort of cliff or spiraled into a wooded area on the dark, rural roads in one of the nearby towns. Flaherty also knew that if something had happened inside that house, the last thing Matterazzo wanted to do was burst in there and disturb a crime scene. If Matterazzo's version of events—that the family had seemingly vanished, leaving behind dirty dishes and a filled bathtub, and their cell phones on the counter—was true, it was a strong possibility that there had been some sort of foul play. Flaherty had certainly seen it before.

"Joe, sit tight. Let me make some calls. In the meantime, don't go in the house. Don't touch anything. I'll get right back to you," Flaherty said, then he proceeded to ask questions about Rachel and Neil, whom he had never met. It was Matterazzo's children from his first marriage whom Flaherty was friendly with. In fact, Joe Matterazzo's son Michael would be the best man at Flaherty's own son's wedding. "By the way, what's up with the husband? Any domestic troubles, any problems there? Any chance he got into a fight with Rachel and she's hurt, and the baby's in England with him?"

"No, he's a good kid. A sharp kid," Matterazzo replied. "He's like an English gentleman, treats Rachel really well. He seems nothing but devoted to her. I never saw them fight. He loves that baby. And he's not exactly the toughest kid I've met. I don't see it."

Flaherty was not convinced. He had seen seemingly secure, happy men snap and wipe out their entire families. There were all too many cases of that sort that had piled up on his desk at the elite CPAC (Crime Prevention and Control) unit of the Suffolk County District Attorney's Office. He hung up with Matterazzo and reached out to another state trooper who had been his counterpart in the Office of the Middlesex District Attorney Jimmy Connolly. Both men had commanded detectives assigned to investigate the most violent cases that came through the district attorney's office, and had even worked a number of murders together. Tough ones too. In fact, one particularly gruesome homicide case came to mind when Flaherty heard Matterazzo talk about his missing step-daughter and her family, but he pushed those thoughts out of his mind so he could focus.

Connolly was out of cell-phone reach and didn't receive the pages that Flaherty was sending out, so he called for the state trooper on duty in the Middlesex DA's office. A short time later, Massachusetts State Police Detective Bobby Manning called him back.

"Bobby. This is Joe Flaherty. Listen, I got a call from a friend of mine worried about his step-daughter and her family," he said, before laying out the scenario that he had heard from Matterazzo: woman who calls her mother every day is nowhere to be found; family just moved into a new house; husband an immigrant. "My friend's a real level-headed guy. It doesn't sound good. Something's up here. Can you help them out?"

Manning agreed to start making phone calls. Then Flaherty called the Hopkinton police to alert them that the Matterazzos were on their way, and offered up any assistance he could give them from the state police level. But by then, the Matterazzos had already arrived and were talking to Sergeant Sutton, the officer who had jimmied the lock open and walked through the Entwistles' house the night before.

Worry had left Priscilla Matterazzo looking haggard, and her husband was practically holding her up with a strong arm around her shoulders as she asked to fill out a missing persons report. Sergeant Sutton was distracted by the sound of a dog barking outside, went to the window, and saw the basset hound he had left locked in a cage the night before on a leash held by Maureen Gately.

"How did you get the dog?" Sutton asked.

Joanna Gately explained that she and her sister had slept in their car outside of 6 Cubs Path waiting for the Entwistles to come home, a wait made in vain. Frantic, she'd begun knocking on doors asking neighbors if anyone had the key to the house. One neighbor remembered that the last occupants had given him the security code to the garage door's push-pad in case of an emergency, and wondered if it would still work. It did. The Gatelys had used the code to get inside the house to take Sally out of her cage.

"The four of them were in a heightened state of alarm," Sutton would later recall. "They were practically begging us to help them."

Sutton directed the foursome to Officer Gregg De-Boer, who would help them with the tedious task of filling out a pile of paperwork about the Entwistles. Another officer, Detective Scott vanRaalten, turned his attention to the family's missing BMW. He called LoJack to see if the Entwistles' vehicle was registered with them. It was not. He called OnStar with the same question. No luck. Even BMW said it could not have a GPS locating device in the SUV, as it was too old a model.

Meanwhile, Sutton and O'Neil returned to Cubs Path and started knocking on doors, asking if anyone had noticed anything suspicious. Of course, the Entwistles had only moved in a week before, so most of the neighbors had not even met the family yet. They had just watched moving trucks pull in and out of the driveway.

Flaherty made another call to Hopkinton police and asked if they would call in a detective on his day off so that an investigator could take the job from start to finish. Ordinarily, a patrol officer would make a report—one of dozens in a single shift—and then wait for a detective to respond. Flaherty knew from experience that if a detective could be on the case from the beginning, make it his, he would care about the outcome a little more than an overworked guy in a patrol car running from one 911 call to another. With Flaherty's call, Hopkinton police began to act with a sense of urgency. It had become clear that the well-being check they had conducted the night before was not just a routine case of an unexplained broken dinner engagement. The panic in the eyes of Rachel's mother and stepfather was enough to raise all the cops' suspicions. Instinct told them to move as if they were investigating a crime scene, even if at that point, they did not know how correct that assumption would be. Detective Scott vanRaalten came in on his day off to work the case, and started by talking to the family himself.

Joanna Gately gave the police the garage code she had gotten from the neighbor. She looked especially nervous, and had a reason other than worry for her anxiety. She did not want to mention it aloud, especially with Rachel's parents nearby, but when she'd gone into the Entwistle house to walk poor Sally, she had been blasted by a foul odor that did not come from the direction of the dog, and was not the smell of an animal's accident. The stench was overwhelming, and one that she had never smelled before. It was so strong it brought bile to the back of her throat. She did not need to be a scientist to detect that the rancid odor was a likely sign that something very bad had happened inside that house.

Sergeant Sutton and Detective vanRaalten got in their car to go to 6 Cubs Path, and Gately stayed behind with the Matterazzos to fill out the police report. She didn't mention the odor.

She didn't need to.

"You smell that?" was the first thing Sutton said out loud, as both cops heard the gears fire up and the squeak of pulleys lifting the garage door. As the door pulled up, the smell hit them in the face like a wet towel on a humid day.

"Yeah. It's like a dirty diaper or something," the detective responded.

The officers followed the smell past the kitchen and began to climb up the stairs. With each step, the stench became more unpleasant. By the time they were on the second floor, both men were holding their hands over their faces to block it out.

Sutton would later write this chilling account in a police report:

> *Upon entry, the officers detected a smell, which, based on their training and experience, suggested a dead body was on the premises. The odor heightened our concern.*

The stench was strongest outside the master bedroom, which they had only viewed from the doorway the day before, and found to "be unkempt, as if someone had slept in the bed, had not made it, and had laid the comforter and other bed linens back on the bed. (They found the bed in the same condition as it was the day before during their earlier walk through.)," Sutton noted.

Detective vanRaalten looked inside the bathroom, saw nothing out of place, and pulled open the door to a walk-in closet.

As vanRaalten searched the outer rooms, Sutton spotted a lady's wristwatch and a pair of eyeglasses on the floor next to the bed, as if someone had slipped them off just before falling asleep. With a feeling of trepidation, he pulled back the left side of the comforter near the foot of the bed and saw a woman's foot, discolored with death. It was not an entirely surprising find, given the smell, but still Sutton yelped.

"You have to see this," he said. VanRaalten had already sprinted to the side of the bed after hearing his supervisor cry out.

In an effort not to disturb any evidence, Sutton carefully gripped a corner of the rumpled comforter near the top of the bed and lifted it straight up as van-Raalten looked underneath. He had to stifle his own cry when he saw the face of a baby, who had "been dead for some time," the detective would later recall. He assumed that it was the smiling 9-month-old who had been reported missing—and whose picture was framed in every room—but he couldn't be positive. Her face was battered, and unrecognizable. Rachel was lying in the fetal position with the baby clutched close to her breasts.

Baby Lillian Rose was lying on her back, cradled next to her mother, also "obviously deceased," Sutton would later write. The manner of death was not immediately apparent. Only when the state medical examiner arrived to move the bodies, and the baby was pulled from her mother, did the cops notice that the little girl had been shot in the stomach. The bullet had passed through her and hit her mother in the torso. There was also a small hole in the center of Rachel's forehead, just above her hairline. In addition to the baby's gunshot wound, something had happened to her face, as if she'd taken a punch or a hard slap that had left clear damage to her soft, white skin. There were bruises around her left eye, her nose and the mouth area, along with blood and mucus that had crusted on her tiny nostrils and lips.

It was an image that would likely haunt both seasoned cops for the rest of their lives.

After they'd found the bodies, Sutton placed the comforter back exactly the way he had found it and realized right away that the mother and daughter had probably been dead the night before when they were there conducting the well-being check.

The thought that he'd missed them made Sutton sick to his stomach.

It was clear, now, that the rumpled bedclothes over their bodies and the pillows over their faces had been placed there intentionally, a desperate move made by the killer to hide the atrocity that he had just committed—maybe even from his own eyes.

HOPKINTON HAD JUST RECORDED the first double homicide committed in the town's long history. In fact, though the sleepy suburb had been involved in a couple of murder investigations, this was the first time the bloodletting had occurred in the town itself.

In 1992, the body of Mary Ann Seguin, 35, wrapped in bloody linens and towels stained with brain matter, had been fished out of the Sudbury River in the Hopkinton State Park after her husband, Kenneth, a successful computer software programmer who'd grown up in the town, killed her with a single hatchet blow to her head as she'd slept in the couple's bed in the neighboring town of Holliston. The discovery set off a desperate search for Kenneth Seguin, and the couple's two children, Amy, 5, and David, 7, who were missing. Hopkinton police were part of that frantic hunt. Every cop involved had prayed that the kids would be found alive—prayers that went unanswered.

Joe Flaherty was one of the investigators who'd made the terrible discovery of the children. Divers had found their bodies in a pond in Franklin, a town outside of Hopkinton. Flaherty had been assigned to work the case for another district attorney's office. To this day, he has been unable to shake the image of the little girl and her big brother being pulled from the murky sludge. Amy's wrists were cut so deeply, her small hands were dangling from her arms. Her brother David had been slashed across the throat with a ferocious wound that nearly severed his head. Their cowardly father had drugged them with over-the-counter sleeping pills that he had mixed into their little juice boxes, then hacked at them with a knife before dumping their bodies.

"I'll never forget it," Flaherty would later remember. "We pulled those bodies out of the pond and when we all saw them . . . all you could hear is this sigh. This massive sigh. The sight of it was shocking. Even on the autopsy table, the kids looked like angels. You couldn't even imagine what was going through their minds as their father did this to them. What was going through his mind?

"Then he goes back in the house, all quiet, like he had just put the kids to bed, picked up an axe and drove it into his wife's head," Flaherty said.

After the killings, Seguin had been found wandering in the woods of Hopkinton State Park with self-inflicted slashes that led to massive blood loss. He denied any involvement with his wife's murder, and told the cops he didn't know where his kids were. It was Kenneth Seguin who'd jumped into Flaherty's mind when Joe Matterazzo called him about the missing family. That case, more than most, showed him that evil can emerge in the most unlikely places.

Just like Neil Entwistle, Seguin was living an idyllic suburban life he could not afford. He was awash in debt and saw killing his wife and family, and himself, as the only way out. But he was too cowardly to perform that last task.

His attorney argued that he was insane. But a jury was unconvinced and convicted him of second-degree murder, a sentence that could make him eligible to be released on parole any day now.

Then, in 1995, police found the body of a 30-year-old prostitute, Marta Santiago, in a Hopkinton field. Santiago, who had recently been released from the Massachusetts Correctional Institution in Framingham after serving a six-month sentence on drug and shoplifting charges, had been beaten and stabbed by a john after she'd told him she was infected with HIV. That man, Domingo Ardon, is serving a life sentence for the slaying. He had worked at a nursery that owned the field in Hopkinton where his victim's body had been dumped.

But it had been more than a decade since any violent crime had been recorded in Hopkinton. The police officers who'd found the bodies of Rachel and Lillian Rose Entwistle were well aware that the discovery would rattle the entire town and become national news. Joe Flaherty felt as though he was reliving the Kenneth Seguin murders—only this time the victims were all too close, not just angels on an autopsy table, but a mother and baby girl who were loved by a man he had been friends with for thirty years.

Flaherty did not want to be the man who broke the

news of the macabre discovery to Joe Matterazzo. Instead, Sutton used his department-issued Nextel to
call Gregg DeBoer, who was still filling out paperwork
with the Matterazzos and the Gately sisters at Hopkinton police headquarters. Sutton asked the officer to
step out of the room so he would not be heard, and
DeBoer complied.

"It appears that the missing woman and her baby
are homicides. Don't let any of them leave until the
chief gets there to make notifications. Don't let them
come here," he ordered. "And keep your mouth shut."

The news was so startling, DeBoer had to tell
someone. So he pulled the police dispatcher aside and
whispered it to her. Then he closed his eyes, said a
silent prayer, pulled open the door of the conference
room and went back to the business of filling out
missing persons reports, even while knowing that two
of the three subjects listed in the paperwork had already been found dead.

Back at 6 Cubs Path, the two officers searched the
rest of the house, looking for Neil. Neither cop really
expected to find him. Both had enough law enforcement experience to know that in any domestic homicide, especially when a child is the victim, the father is
the prime suspect. As sickening as it was to imagine a
father firing a .22-caliber bullet into the chest of his
own baby, both officers knew that there was a strong
possibility that that was exactly what had happened.

Shooting babies is extremely rare. In 2005, the FBI
released research that said that most infanticides—
two-thirds, in fact—were committed by hand. Un-
leashing a bullet into a baby's body was unusually

savage, even by the standards of the most brutal killers or enraged jilted lovers.

DETECTIVE VANRAALTEN HAD CALLED Chief Thomas Irvin at home. Irvin put on his dress blues and drove to the station to perform what is the worst part of police work for any officer: delivering the terrible news to the victims' loved ones. It's an onerous duty under any circumstances, but watching Priscilla Matterazzo fall to the floor with the weight of her grief, while her husband twitched with his own pain, was something that Chief Irvin will never, ever forget.

As the chief tried to comfort the family, Sutton broadcast a message over his police radio, his breath shallow with anger, his words clipped by the rage:

"We are looking for a white male. Neil Entwistle. He may be driving a 2004 white BMW. Repeat. We are looking for a white male in a white BMW Mass. Reg. six-five-Kerry-Walter-seven-nine. Consider him armed."

Within minutes, the snow-crusted Colonial at 6 Cubs Path was crawling with cops. Forensic investigators with the vaunted Crime Scene Services Section and the homicide unit of the Massachusetts State Police assigned to the Office of the Middlesex District Attorney began to move methodically through the house. Despite their numbers, the mood inside was eerily quiet as each officer went about the task of carefully cataloging every piece of evidence. No one spoke of the smell. Some, especially those with their own babies at home, made a silent vow to themselves to spend extra time with their children that night.

Outside, reporters stood behind yellow crime-scene tape hurtling questions at confused neighbors and spectators who had seen the commotion and come to stare at the chaos of swirling police lights and TV trucks. None of the neighbors had ever spoken to the young family, but some recalled seeing Rachel proudly pushing her baby around the neighborhood in a carriage, or spotted Neil pulling out of the driveway in a sporty BMW. Other than that the Entwistles were strangers.

"It absolutely doesn't fit the community," one neighbor, John Hankard, told reporters, shaking his head sadly as he spoke. "This would be the last place that anyone who knows the town would ever think this would happen."

Chief Irvin tried to assuage the panic in the town by telling reporters that the murders were an anomaly. "This is a quiet, professional neighborhood of working families and schoolchildren that we would normally consider as safe," he said. "There is no reason to fear that there will be a repetition of this."

Neil Entwistle wouldn't have the guts for it, Irvin thought but didn't say.

News photographers wrapped themselves in warm clothing, knowing that it would be a long wait in the frigid cold before they could make the requisite grim picture of the medical examiner's van as it carried out the bodies of the victims. The temperature was in the low teens, and it got even colder towards the morning side of midnight. Exhaust pipes on all the news vans sprayed fumes as TV reporters kept warm inside with engines running. Most of the people assembled inside and outside the Entwistle home might have seemed too casual about the horror to those whose lives are not filled with bloodshed, those who have become somewhat cynical about crime. Some might even say callous. But the truth was that, after years of respond-ing to bloody scenes or reporting about carnage, crime reporters, forensic investigators and homicide cops develop an internal defense against emotionaliz-ing the atrocities that they witness on a daily basis. They have to, so their own lives are not consumed with other people's grief.

Despite that built-in defense mechanism, not a sin-gle person inside or outside 6 Cubs Path that day would ever wipe out the memory of a medical exam-iner pushing an adult-sized stretcher containing a zipped-up baby-sized body bag. The sight was espe-cially startling for those who had seen the photo-graphs of Rachel and her daughter that were already displayed on tables or on the walls in the Entwistles' new house, pictures that cataloged the first nine months in the life of an undeniably beautiful baby girl and the joy of motherhood for a beloved young schoolteacher.

CHAPTER 7

THE PHONE CALL THAT came just before 7 p.m. on Sunday, January 22, spurred the investigators in Troop F at Boston's Logan International Airport into action. A follow-up call from Joe Flaherty telling them the urgent nature of the request solidified in everyone's mind that the task they were about to undertake was an important one. Flaherty was well-known and well-respected. If he had a hand in this, even though he was retired, it was serious business.

Many in Troop F were grateful to be pulled into an investigation, however tragic. All of the troopers wore badges swathed in black bands of mourning. Just months earlier, one of their own, State Trooper Vincent Cila, an eighteen-year veteran of the state police who had a wife and two little girls, had died in an on-duty motorcycle crash in Boston's Tip O'Neill Tunnel, leaving many of his fellow troopers with a lingering sense of malaise. Jumping into a murder investigation was a good way to pull Troop F out of their funk.

The troop's commander began to outline what his

investigators were expected to look for. There was a BOLO—Be on the Lookout—for a white male named Neil Entwistle, six-foot-one, 200 pounds with brown eyes, brown hair and a light complexion. If he could not be located, then Hopkinton police wanted to find his car, a 2004 white BMW SUV, more evidence that the prime suspect in the slaughter had indeed fled the country.

It took just forty-five minutes for the state troopers to come through. They had located the vehicle in one of the many sprawling parking lots that are spread out through Logan. It had been parked in the West Garage Level Area DD since 10:49 p.m. on Saturday night—just hours after the Gatelys showed up at the Entwistle home and found no one there. Airport security cameras had captured Neil pulling into the same garage at 8:14 p.m. but he vacated it for some reason at 9:34. Investigators would later learn that he had driven to several automatic teller machines, where he desperately tried to pull cash advances from a number of different credit cards. Then he purchased a small amount of gas on Route 9 near the Chestnut Hill Mall in Boston, just enough to get him back to the airport. He pulled back in at 10:49 p.m.

When state troopers found the vehicle, the doors were locked and the keys were dangling from the ignition. There was another set inside that would be identified as the keys to his in-laws' house in Carver. The driver's side seat was in the reclined position. The roof racks were empty. There was a Dasani water bottle in the cup holder. And there was a baby seat strapped in the rear.

Within minutes, investigators swarmed British Airways, the most likely airline for a native of England, and found that a man named Neil Entwistle had indeed used a Visa debit card to buy a one-way ticket to London for the 2:38 p.m. flight that would leave Boston Sunday afternoon. But a seat had opened on an earlier flight.

By 8:15 a.m. Neil Entwistle had boarded a British Airways flight with no luggage whatsoever and flown back across the pond.

CHAPTER 8

THE SOUND OF THE British voice on the other end of the phone Monday morning made Joseph Matterazzo sick. He hadn't slept in days and was fueled by angry adrenaline. He and Priscilla had been kept awake by anxiety, each trying to pray that the news from the day before had been some sort of mistake. The only thing keeping them both going in those long, terrible hours was the work of helping investigators find both the killer and a motive for the crime. To that end, Priscilla Matterazzo gave detectives statements from Rachel's bank accounts, and pointed to the $18,000 in student loan debt her daughter had acquired. She handed over the bogus "ENT" business card Neil had given to her just a few weeks earlier. Then she remembered that Neil had used the computer at her home on January 16, the last time the couple was there, and gave the police permission to search it. A PalmPilot that was found at 6 Cubs Path was also entered into evidence, as were two laptop computers left behind and a pile of data storage disks.

The couple had been busy all morning, and the

phone was ringing off the hook with calls from heart-broken friends and family. Seeped in exhaustion and rage, when Joe Matterazzo heard a British accent on the other end of the call he answered at 11:30 a.m., he tried to compose himself to hear what kind of excuse Cliff Entwistle could come up with for his lowlife of a son.

"I'm sorry to worry you, but I received a disturbing phone call from Neil last night. He told me that something terrible had happened to Rachel and the baby."

Matterazzo could not be positive that Neil was the triggerman in the murders of his step-daughter and granddaughter, though with every hour, Neil was increasingly looking like the prime suspect. Even with the very slim likelihood that he was innocent, what kind of man could flee the country when his wife and baby had been found dead?

"What did Neil tell you?" Matterazzo asked, careful not to give away too much to the father of the man he believed was a monster.

"He said he had gone out for twenty minutes on Friday morning, that he found his wife and daughter in the bedroom, that he called the police, and police arrived at the house," Cliff Entwistle said. "When police got there, he said he drove to your house, but you were not there. He was confused, trying to piece things together. He said it got to the point he couldn't face you, so he drove to the airport, called me and said he wanted to come home," Entwistle said. "He landed a while ago."

Knowing full well that Neil had never called the police on Friday—no one did that day—Matterazzo's fury began to shorten his breath. Either Neil had lied to his own parents, or Cliff Entwistle was lying to him.

"Where's Neil now?" Matterazzo asked.

"He's not here," Entwistle answered. "I don't know where he is."

Matterazzo hung up the phone, disgusted. He called the state police and recounted the conversation, then sat back down at the kitchen table with his head in his hands. He could not get the screaming in his head to stop. When the phone rang again, he picked it up with a barked "*Hello!*"

"Joe. It's Neil," he heard.

Then there was a long, still silence as Matterazzo tried to contain his rage.

"Listen, Joe, I'm sorry. I don't know what happened. I went out, and then when I came back, I found them like that. I don't know what happened."

"Really, Neil?" Matterazzo snarled. "You might want to tell that story to the investigators."

Then he slammed down the phone. Joe Flaherty had been spending much of his time at the Matterazzos' home in the hours since the murders were discovered. He heard the slam of the phone into the cradle and cautioned Matterazzo that it could only help to talk to Neil, to punch holes in the stories that he was certain to start spinning from the safety of his home turf back in England.

"Keep him on the phone. I know you want to kill him. But keep him on the phone. Everything he says can be used against him," Flaherty cautioned Matterazzo.

By then, media hordes from around the world had

picked up the horrific story of the young mom and her baby girl murdered in an upscale suburban community in a placid part of New England. Middlesex District Attorney Martha Coakley's office was getting inundated with phone calls about the missing father and husband, but would only say that Neil Entwistle was "a person of interest" in the case.

On January 24, 2006—the Tuesday after the bodies were found—Coakley's office sent out a press release about their findings.

The Office of the Chief Medical Examiner (ME) has completed its autopsies on the bodies of a 27-year old woman and her 9-month-old daughter, who were found dead in their Hopkinton home Sunday evening. While initially investigators only detected one gunshot wound to Rachel Entwistle's torso, autopsy revealed that the cause of death was a gunshot wound to the head. The ME found the cause of death of 9-month-old Lillian Entwistle to be a single gunshot wound to the abdomen. Both deaths were ruled homicides.

There was no mention of the bruises that covered Lillian Rose's tiny face. Or of the fact that the bodies were missed the first time Hopkinton police had conducted the "well-being search," an embarrassing fact for the town's law enforcement officials.

"Additionally," the statement read,

investigators located a BMW belonging to Neil Entwistle, Ms. Entwistle's husband. . . . In addi-

tion, police have been in contact with Mr. En-
twistle, who is out of the country. No further
information as to his whereabouts is being re-
leased at this time. . . . Mr. Entwistle is still
considered a person of interest in the investi-
gation.

As hard as Coakley tried to contain the information, by the time her office released that statement, it
had already been leaked that Neil Entwistle was in
England. It didn't take a genius to figure out that he
would have gone home anyway. Both the *Boston Herald* and the *Boston Globe* had dispatched reporters to
his gritty hometown to try to find him. Producers
from television news outlets were crowding flights to
London.

There would be no containing this story, even if it
was all too familiar, to the American public at least,
who had watched the case of a handsome pesticides
salesman named Scott Peterson, who had reported his
wife, Laci, eight months pregnant, missing from their
California home on Christmas Eve in 2002, and then
had the gall to appeal to his neighbors for help in finding the woman he had slain. Her body, and the body
of their baby boy Conner, were found separately in
the spring of 2003 about three miles from the spot
where Scott Peterson told investigators he had been
fishing when his wife vanished.

Just like Neil Entwistle, Scott Peterson had wooed
Laci's family. He seemed like nothing but a loving
husband who was eager for the birth of the couple's
first child. He wasn't even considered a suspect for

the first few months after his wife disappeared, largely because her family considered him a man devastated by loss, never imagining that he was actually a manipulative, calculating killer who had been cheating on Laci with another woman. On April 18, 2003, Peterson was arrested on a fancy golf course in California carrying a wad of cash, his brother's driver's license, and credit cards belonging to his family members. He had dyed his hair blonde and was toting several knives. Police believed he was getting set to flee to Mexico.

Just months before Rachel and Lillian Entwistle were murdered, a California jury had convicted Scott Peterson of murdering his wife and baby, saying that it was his "myriad of lies" that convinced then he was guilty. A California judge, Alfred Delucchi, said that Peterson was "cruel, uncaring, heartless and callous" and sentenced him to death by lethal injection. Right now, Peterson is appealing those charges.

Unlike Scott Peterson, no one thought Neil Entwistle was innocent. Rachel's family was certainly not rallying behind him in support. As reporters began to gather outside the Matterazzos' house in Carver, Flaherty had begun to act as the family's press contact. Flaherty's own wife, Nina, had been a spokesperson for the Norfolk County Office of the District Attorney, and had experience dealing with reporters during a crisis. The Matterazzos, and Rachel's brother, Jerome Souza, released a statement through Flaherty that made no mention of Neil at all. "The entire family is overwhelmed by the loss of Rachel and Lillian and the events of last weekend. . . . As the family continues to grieve, we also celebrate and are grateful for the time we had with Rachel and Lilly," Flaherty told the press at his Cambridge law office. After retirement, Flaherty, who is also an attorney, opened a private firm.

"We are also grateful for the outpouring of prayers, love and support offered by family, friends and strangers alike," the statement continued. "Rachel was a wonderful wife, daughter, granddaughter, sister and mother. With the birth of Rachel's daughter, Lillian Rose Entwistle, last April, Rachel shared her greatest love, that of being a mother.

"We will take Rachel and Lillian to their rest," Flaherty said, urging the press to respect the family's privacy. "The family has every confidence that the Middlesex County district attorney's office—Martha Coakley's office—along with the Massachusetts State Police and the Hopkinton Police Department, will solve this case and bring to justice those responsible."

Neil was also excluded from Rachel and Lillian's death notices that appeared in the Quincy *Patriot Ledger*, a local newspaper that served the South Shore of Boston. The notices listed as surviving relatives only "the loving Matterazzo, Cooke and Souza families, as well as many dear family members, both here and in England." No mention of Rachel's husband or Lillian's father. No mention of the terrible way the two had died.

As Priscilla Matterazzo planned the funeral for her daughter and granddaughter, Neil Entwistle remained in England—talking to investigators back in Massachusettts via telephone as he stayed in seclusion at his parents' tidy house. State Trooper Michael Banks spent two hours on the phone in one conversation he had with Neil, who made statements that cast doubt on the stories he had already told his own father.

"Neil Entwistle, this is State Police Trooper Michael Banks. I need to take a statement from you about what happened at Six Cubs Path in Hopkinton, Massachusetts, between the January nineteenth, 2006, and January twenty-second, 2006."

"Sir," Neil said, his voice trembling, "I woke up on Friday [January 20], fed Lilly and left the house a couple hours later to do some errands. I went to Staples, headed to Wal-Mart, but never made it, then came back to the house around eleven a.m."

Neil could not explain why he'd never made it to Wal-Mart, or how he'd spent the two hours he claimed to be away from the home that morning.

"I left the garage door up, so I came in through the garage to the basement door. It was closed, but not locked."

"What kind of condition was the house in when you got back?" Banks asked.

"The same as when I left."

What next? Banks asked.

"I went upstairs and checked the baby's room. She wasn't in there. I didn't hear her crying, and I couldn't find Rachel. I went into my bedroom and saw Rachel, she had a comforter over her. I pulled it back, and Rachel was pale, real pale.

"There was blood on the baby, the baby had been shot. They were dead," Neil said, as he began to cry.

"I pulled the covers back over them and left the

room," Neil said, as a transcript of the conversation would show.

Then what? Banks asked.

Neil described to the trooper how he'd run downstairs and "grabbed a knife from the kitchen" to kill himself, but put it down because it would "hurt too much."

Banks hid his emotions, but would later tell friends he was thinking: *Fucking coward.*

Neil told the trooper that he'd then driven to Carver to tell his in-laws "what had happened."

Why, Banks asked during the interview, hadn't Neil called them on the phone?

"I didn't have their number."

Investigators would later accuse Neil Entwistle of building a myriad of lies, stories that would likely be used against him in court. But it was what he told Banks next that gave police the physical evidence that they planned to use to prove that it was Neil who had shot Rachel and Lillian.

"I was also going to go to Carver to get Joe [Matterazzo]'s gun," Neil said. "I wanted to shoot myself. But no one was there and I couldn't get into his house. I was going to go to Priscilla's job, but I couldn't remember how to get there.

"I drove to the airport and walked around a bit, left and then drove back to Hopkinton, but ended up buying gas, and went back to the airport. I wanted to go home and be with my parents," Neil said.

Banks asked Neil if there had been anything awry in his marriage, if there had been problems.

"I'm unemployed, but I have been looking for full-time work. Believe me, I need it, because the bills are piling up and we have this house I can't afford," Neil said. "I had a job interview scheduled for Friday, but it didn't work out. I didn't tell Rachel. I've been working with a recruiting agency."

Banks would also note that Neil said he had "done some selling on eBay."

"We used to live in England, and I worked doing military research. We came back here in September. I wanted to try and live in both countries, but Rachel wanted to be in the United States so she could be closer to her mother. Rachel wanted Lillian to be raised as an American and be close to her grandmother."

When Banks hung up the phone, he immediately went to work on an affidavit that would point out the obvious flaws in Neil Entwistle's rambling. He'd said he didn't have keys to the Matterazzos' house, but then they found the keys in the BMW. He'd said he saw the bullet holes and blood—evidence that experienced investigators did not detect until the baby's body had been moved. He had told his father he called the police, when he certainly did not. There were holes in the timeline of the morning of the murders when Neil inexplicably did not make it to Wal-Mart, where there are security cameras on the front door. Trooper Banks thought about Neil's story that he had picked up a puny kitchen knife and stared at it, contemplating suicide, before putting it back in the block because "it would hurt too much." That last thought stayed with him as he began working on his affidavit, which would become critical in obtaining a warrant for the arrest of Neil Entwistle on charges of murder.

Banks, who had unraveled the motives for way too many murders, had developed a strong theory about the double homicide a hunch with plenty of circumstantial evidence to bear it out:

> *Based on . . . my training and experience in homicide investigation, I believe that there may be financial motivation for this murder. It appears that Neil and Rachel Entwistle had accumulated a sizeable amount of debt and may have been living well beyond their means, even up until the week of the murders when thousands of dollars worth of furniture, purchased on credit, was delivered to the Entwistle's home, which they were leasing for $2,700 per month. Neil Entwistle had not been working since returning to the United States in September of 2005, and does not appear to have been successful in securing steady income or employment. By his own admission, he needed money to pay for their monthly rent. In addition, this debt, along with Neil Entwistle's secrecy about the status of his work history and the family finances, appears to have caused strain in their relationship, and by itself is indication to me of serious financial problems in the family which gave Neil Entwistle a motive to murder his wife and child.*

There was something else nagging at Banks about the interview, and he went back over his notes, scrawled on a yellow legal pad. When he found what he was looking for, he underlined the words: "Joe's gun."

CHAPTER 9

WHEN INVESTIGATORS TOLD JOE Matterazzo that an autopsy finished just days after the funerals had revealed that the bullets that killed Rachel and Lillian were .22-caliber, his hands began to shake. He quietly rushed to the bedroom where he stashed the lockbox that held his weapons and made sure the small gun was still there. It was. But his relief would be temporary.

The autopsy results were startling. Rachel Entwistle had been shot in the forehead, just above the hairline in the center. Lillian Entwistle had died from a gunshot wound to the abdomen that had passed through her body and entered her mother's torso. According to the autopsy, Rachel had died instantly from the shot to the head, but the bullet that hurtled through the baby's stomach had worked more slowly, meaning little Lilly had suffered in pain spooned next to her mother's dead body.

The bullet that had gone through the baby was intact when it was removed from her mother's stomach. The one that smashed into Rachel's head had broken into two pieces upon impact. But the entry wounds were so small that Neil's contention that he'd seen his wife and baby shot by intruders when he lifted the covers off the bed was appearing to be very unlikely. Even Sergeant Sutton, who'd discovered the bodies, was not entirely sure how the mother and baby died until the medical examiner lifted Lillian away from Rachel's side.

The autopsy results, along with Neil's revelation that he'd planned to drive to his mother-in-law's house and take her husband's gun to kill himself, suggested to investigators that the Matterazzos may have inadvertently played a role in the deaths. Detectives drove directly to the Matterazzos' home and began asking questions about Joe's arsenal. Matterazzo told investigators he was a gun enthusiast, and had a "number of firearms, including a .22-caliber revolver and a rifle." He did keep the guns in his master bedroom, securely locked, but the keys were in plain sight on a countertop in the couple's home. There were no children living there whom they had to worry would play with the keys and find the box, but they did not want to take any unnecessary chances either. Neil and Rachel had had the run of the house. Neil knew exactly where the keys to the lockbox were kept, from the afternoon he'd spent target-shooting with the Matterazzo men. The Entwistles had been visiting the house on January 16, just days before the murders. Never did Joe Matterazzo imagine that he would have to watch Neil's every move in the house that both couples had shared all summer.

So yes, Matterazzo told investigators, it was very

feasible that Neil Entwistle had stolen a gun from his house, used it, and put it back.

What was more troubling still was that Joseph Matterazzo had spent Saturday afternoon—the day that the Entwistle family was first reported missing— firing the .22, and other guns, at target practice with his sons Michael and Anthony, whiling away time because his wife had planned to go to Rachel's house for brunch, and to see the baby. It disgusted him to think that he might have held the same weapon, the very same gun that just hours earlier had been fired by the monster who'd murdered his step-daughter and granddaughter. He had pulled the same trigger that had discharged the fatal blasts that killed them.

Eventually, DNA tests conducted on Matterazzo's .22 would confirm his deep-rooted fear: it was in fact his very own weapon that provided the means and the ammunition that would blow apart his family's life.

Joe would break down to Flaherty, his longtime friend. "We trusted him. We had no idea this secret life he was living. This fucking betrayal . . . To think he drove here where he has always been invited and treated like a member of the family, grabbed my gun, and then came back here to put it back . . . It's just . . ."

With that, Matterazzo stopped talking to his friend and that thought that had replayed over and over in his head for weeks now began to repeat itself: *I wish I had shot this fucking little fairy myself. I really do.*

Investigators had obtained a warrant to take a sample of Neil's DNA from the Dasani water bottle that they had found in the BMW's cup holder. They compared it to DNA found on the grip of the .22 taken from Matterazzo's collection. Of course, Matterazzo's DNA, as well as his sons', was also found. The conclusion would eventually provide the basis of a murder case against Neil Entwistle: the DNA on the grip was a match to his own. The statistical probability of the DNA match not being Entwistle's is 1 in 5.299 trillion.

Investigators believe that he'd shot Rachel at such a close range, there was a blowback of blood and brain matter on the weapon itself—as forensic scientists would discover when studying the DNA recovered from the gun.

Rachel's DNA on the muzzle of her stepfather's .22 proved that it was the weapon used in the slaying, because she had never touched the gun before. Besides, the statistical probability of that DNA match was approximately 1 in 21.82 quadrillion, forensic experts would say.

Worse still, it appeared as if Joseph Matterazzo had taught the killer how to use it.

CHAPTER 10

THE BRITISH PRESS DID not want to believe that one of their countrymen had committed the atrocity of shooting a baby girl to death. While domestic violence is statistically not as common in Europe as it is in the United States, it is still, sadly, not startling if a husband acts like a "nutter" and does his wife in. But killing one's baby in such a cold-hearted way was hard to accept, so stories in England tried to cast doubt on Neil's guilt.

And it remained fresh in the minds of many in England that Entwistle was being tried by Middlesex District Attorney Martha Coakley, who just years earlier had prosecuted a young British au pair, Louise Woodward, on charges of murdering a baby in her care—a controversial case that to this day many Brits believe was the overzealous American prosecution of a vulnerable and naïve teenaged girl on behalf of a wealthy and influential family. The emotional trial became a televised media circus in Massachusetts, much like the O. J. Simpson murder case in Los Angeles.

Woodward had even hired one of Simpson's attorneys, Barry Scheck, to defend her.

Coakley, a stern-looking woman with a penchant for tight power suits and high-heeled pumps, successfully argued that Woodward was a flight risk and should be held without bail at a maximum security prison for women. Then she handed the reins Assistant District Attorney Gerald Leone Jr., who went to work building a case against the English teen that largely relied on proving that she was a party animal who cared more about seeing the play *Rent* in the city than taking care of a toddler and an infant in the suburbs of Newton.

"The Nanny Case," as it was quickly dubbed by the media, centered around the death of Matthew Eappen, an 8-month-old baby who'd died in Woodward's care on February 9, 1997, five days after being admitted to the hospital. For four of those days, little Matthew was kept alive with machines until his parents, Sunil and Deborah Eappen, had to make the painful decision to let him go. Forensic experts said the baby had died of a fractured skull and subdural hematoma, injuries often detected in shaken babies. He'd also had a fractured wrist that had gone unnoticed for more than a month. Woodward was charged with manslaughter shortly after she told Newton police that she had "popped the baby on the bed." Shortly before the baby died, Woodward had also told another au pair whom she had befriended that Matthew "didn't look right . . . he was off-color, kind of blue." She would later admit that she'd panicked, yelled Matthew's name, and shaken him slightly to see if he would respond to her. The baby vomited on her, but would never wake up. Prosecutors were convinced he'd died of shaken baby syndrome.

A month after the murder allegation, Louise Woodward passed a lie detector test when asked if she had caused any injuries to the boy in her care. But Coakley tried her on first-degree murder charges in a case called *Massachusetts* vs. *Louis Woodward* that would be shown on Court TV. It would infuriate many English people. Prosecutors painted Woodward as a reckless teenager whose booze-fueled nights out partying left her unable to care for children. Her friends were put on the stand, and they testified that Woodward had ceaselessly complained of the curfew that the Eappens had imposed on her, and that she had grown tired of the "baby crying all the time."

The defense argued that Matthew could have had a lingering injury—like the undetected broken wrist—that ultimately caused his death. They presented evidence of a possible gender disorder. There were also hints that the baby's older brother, Brendan, may have hurt his sibling while playing, causing the fatal injury.

Spectators on both sides of the Atlantic were riveted to the televised trial. A jury deliberated for thirty hours before finding Louise Woodward guilty of second-degree murder. The pudgy aspiring actress began to weep in her attorney's arms when the verdict was read. The next morning at her sentencing she blurted through tears, "I don't know what happened to him. I didn't kill Matthew Eappen." But second-degree murder carries a sentence of life in prison with the possibility of parole after fifteen years. Outrage erupted in England as the teen was sent back to prison in tears.

A month later, in a stunning decision, Judge Hiller Zobel reduced Louise Woodward's conviction to involuntary manslaughter, and sentenced her to 279 days in prison, the time she had already served. She was forced to remain in the United States until the appeal made by Coakley and Leone could be heard in the Supreme Court.

Months later, Zobel's ruling was held up by the high court, and by June of 1998 Louise Woodward was free to go home to Elton, England. When she landed on European soil, she was greeted with a heroine's welcome, wooed by talk show host Martin Bashir on the famed show *Panorama* and greeted by camera crews in the town's local pub. It would take years for her to settle into a semi-normal existence after attending law school in England. In 2007, Louise Woodward announced to an English magazine writer that she had fallen in love, planned to marry and would definitely have her own children.

Just months after Woodward announced her intention to become a mother in the magazine *Closer*, a Boston law magazine called *Exhibit A* highlighted her as well, as one of one of the top ten most notorious criminals in the state of Massachusetts. The distinction prompted her attorney, Elaine Whitfield Sharp, to huff, "This shows the American hysteria over this case is never going to go away." She should know. Whitfield Sharp had been pulled over for drunk driving in Massachusetts after Woodward returned home, and was said to have told a state trooper, *Everyone knew she was guilty.* Whitfield Sharp would later deny saying that.

So there was lingering resentment in the British press about the way Middlesex District Attorney Martha Coakley had prosecuted one of their own, and now she was setting her sights on another working-class native of England. The tabloids began to spin theories that Rachel and Lillian Entwistle had been murdered in revenge executions for the Internet scams the couple had been running. One week after the murder, when investigators were still trying to talk to Neil Entwistle about the case, a reporter for the English newspaper spun this theory about the double homicide on the front page, casting doubt on Massachusetts law enforcement officials' insistence that Neil Entwistle was a "person of interest":

WAS PERFECT FAMILY VICTIM OF VENDETTA?

As grieving father in Boston "execution" case is released after a day of questioning, the discovery of threatening e-mails suggests his wife was the target of a hate campaign

Police are investigating the Entwistles' business interests, which encompassed an address in York and another in London's Clerkenwell, along with interests in the murky world of internet pornography and get-rich-quick schemes. Officers said that the family could have had formidable enemies.

The story pointed out that Neil did not have a criminal record, "not even a driving offense," and stressed that Nottingham police in England were denying that their countryman was a suspect at all. The piece also showed sympathy for Neil:

> *What appears certain is that Entwistle has been left profoundly traumatised by the loss of the daughter and the bubbly American brunette he met at the University of York rowing club.*

Other stories repeatedly pointed to the website where a ripped-off customer wrote, "Rachel Entwistle is a bitch," giving the British press plenty of fodder to bolster the beliefs of some that Rachel and Lillian Entwistle were killed by a hit man furious that he had been robbed.

Entwistle's promise on eBay to turn customers into potential "millionaires" was beginning to unravel. One victim, David Brown of Coalville, Leicestershire, England, complained that he'd mailed in a large payment for computer software, but the product had never arrived:

> *The advert went along the lines of rather than the promotion company spending $20,000 on advertising in computer magazines, they were selling massively reduced original program copies at a fraction of the price you would normally pay. I thought the advert was pretty genuine at the time. I suppose all the other losers thought the same too, eh?*

In a comment left on the board, Brown called Rachel Entwistle a "liar" and a "thief." Brown was interviewed by the investigators, but the execution theory never did pick up steam in the United States.

Martha Coakley would continue to insist that Neil Entwistle was not the only killer being considered. In one press conference she emphatically stated:

"Neil Entwistle, husband of Rachel and father of Lillian, remains a person of interest in this investigation. No one has been ruled in and no one has been ruled out as a suspect in this investigation. A person of interest is a person who we believe may have relevant information about the case that we are investigating.

"This is a very active investigation, and is in fact operating twenty-four hours a day at this time. Investigators are making consistent progress on several fronts; however, there are still many pieces of this puzzle missing," she rambled. "It is important to note that no arrest warrants have been issued.

"There are a number of individuals—friends, family, former colleagues and other acquaintances—in both the United States and the United Kingdom, with whom the police are interested in speaking as the investigation proceeds. These deaths are not considered random, and there were no signs forced entry at the residence in Hopkinton where the victims were found."

That last point, along with the fact that Neil had fled the country, cemented the idea in the minds of many that he was the only person with the method and the motive to have killed his wife and baby.

It would be hard to convince anyone that Neil

Entwistle was innocent of the horrendous crime, especially after the highly publicized funeral of Rachel and Lillian.

He was not among the mourners. In fact, he had called authorities from England and relinquished any control of his wife and daughter's bodies to his in-laws.

In all likelihood, tensions would have been high had the man who admitted he fled the country after discovery of the bloody corpses of Rachel and Lillian attended their services. How could a man not show up to a funeral Mass said for his own wife and baby girl?

CHAPTER 11

PRISCILLA MATTERAZZO WAS COMPLETELY numb as she sat in the front pew at St. Peter's Church in Plymouth on February 1, 2006. Not crying. Not angry. Barely breathing. It was as if someone had stuffed her into a small hole and then blotted out all the light. She was completely unaware of the mourners packed into the church dabbing at tears. She was oblivious to the priest's soft voice, even, as Father William MacKenzie tried to make sense of the senseless: "Hold dear the memories of Rachel and Lillian, share love among one another to ease the sorrow of these saddest of days." She could not even feel the strong grip of her husband's hand on her trembling leg.

Just in front of her was something no mother, no grandmother, should ever have to contemplate: a single wooden casket holding the bodies of Rachel and Lilly, lying together forever in the same way that they were found—with the mother cradling her baby girl to her chest. Priscilla Matterazzo and other loved ones had prayed around it, holding hands and sobbing before the funeral Mass began, but Priscilla had clenched her eyes shut as she stood there. Not wanting to look.

The coffin was in front of the same altar where just seven weeks earlier, Lillian Rose Entwistle had been baptized in an idyllic ceremony. All had been perfect that day. The church was beautiful, whitewashed wood and a tall steeple that could be seen from miles around. Priscilla could not shake the image of Neil holding up his daughter with a proud grin stretching across his face as Rachel smiled nearby, looking complete—which was all Priscilla ever wanted for her daughter. Fulfillment. That day, the Entwistles had seemed the perfect family, and Priscilla had felt blessed, grateful even.

The words she heard from Rachel's former classmate were all a blur. It was as if the woman were talking about someone else: "Rachel was a true friend. She loved nature. When we were kids, she was going to be a Supreme Court Justice. A surgeon." The woman recalled a teacher at their Silver Lake Regional High School telling them, "the best of you will become teachers." And Rachel was one of the best of them. She loved Henry David Thoreau. Walks. Talks with her friends.

IN ENGLAND, RACHEL'S FORMER students held their own memorial—thousands of miles away from the Massachusetts church where she was being remembered. More than 600 people crammed into the St. Augustine's Catholic High School theater, carrying *sprays of* winter flowers and leaving notes on a table piled high with hand-scrawled messages next to a silver-framed photograph of their former teacher smiling and holding her baby daughter. The picture was flanked by pink lilies and carnations.

Neil's image had clearly been cropped from the photo.

"Enty and Lilly, you are in my thoughts, love Jessica," read one of the notes. Others asked the question that would be raised by Father Michael Dolman, who celebrated the memorial Mass for Rachel in England: "How can someone with so much vitality, so much to give, meet such a tragic and violent end? We have so many questions. There are no easy answers."

Four of "Enty's" students came forward after the priest spoke to lay offerings on the altar next to her photograph. One carried an English textbook that Rachel had used with them during their studies; a second presented a large leather-bound condolence book that would be sent to Rachel's heartbroken family; the third and fourth students gingerly carried a folded American flag symbolizing what fellow teacher Chris Marples described as "her American background, in particular her Boston roots."

As the Mass came to a close, mourners were struck by the imagery of nine of Rachel Entwistle's drama students clad in matching black dresses, their eyes rimmed and swollen from sleepless nights and shed tears. The girls looked at one another as each clutched a single red rose, and began to sing an a capella rendition of "Because You Loved Me," a Celine

Dion song that moved many of the assembled students to tears.

BACK IN MASSACHUSETTS, RACHEL Entwistle's classmates, who had befriended her when she was the same age as her students in England, began to speak. As they shared memories, Priscilla stared at Jesus Christ hanging from the cross above the priest's head and thought: *Why?* The answer would not come that day, but she would take a small bit of peace from the glow of the sunlight that streamed through the church's stained-glass windows, warming her face. She was also soothed by the soprano voices of two men as they sang the lullaby "All Through the Night," which begins:

> *Sleep my child and peace attend thee,*
> *All through the night*
> *Guardian angels God will send thee,*
> *All through the night*

Even with the sun on her face and the warmth of the lyrics, Priscilla's skin felt cold and clammy. She pulled her blue coat closer to her and moved a bit nearer to Joe. Everything seemed so dark—even with the kind words from the people who eulogized Rachel. Even with the comforting prayers of the family priest. Even with the love of her husband and son who flanked her.

"Never ask why God allowed this to happen," the priest cautioned the more than 500 mourners who crammed into the church, and spilled outside into the cold air where his sermon was heard over speakers. "Because God did not do this."

God's plan is often "frustrated by the evil that lives among us," he said.

"It was only seven weeks ago that we gathered in this same place to celebrate and pray at Lillian's baptism, to pray that she would always remain close to the Lord. Now we are gathered for the saddest of times," the priest said. "There will be people who will wonder why it is God's will that we are gathered today, why it is His will that there is so much sadness.

"It is not God's will. God will weep for us. God will be sad for us."

Reverend MacKenzie never mentioned Neil. No one did. The collage of photographs of Rachel and Lillian that decorated the funeral home for their wake the nights before did not include a single image of Neil. It was as if Rachel's husband and Lillian's father had never even existed.

Priscilla Matterazzo certainly wished he had never been born. She could not believe she had embraced that man as a son. She had that thought over and over—the one she had already expressed aloud to her husband—as her family followed that horrible hearse carrying her daughter and granddaughter to Evergreen Cemetery in Kingston, the town where Rachel had attended high school. *Goddamn it, Neil. We showed you nothing but love.* With Joe behind her, holding her up, his gray hair slicked back, sporting a neatly clipped goatee, Priscilla leaned into his gray trench coat and began to shake. She stood at the hole that had been dug for the shared grave and slipped into a kind of shock that some were afraid she would never recover from.

CHAPTER 12

TROOPER MICHAEL BANKS HAD only spoken to Neil Entwistle over the phone. Hopkinton Detective Scott vanRaalten had only seen pictures of the suspect he had dubbed *son of a bitch*, at least privately. In February 2006, the two would travel to England to interview the man prosecutors were still calling a "person of interest" in the case. They had traveled to England once before, on January 25, five days after the killings of Rachel and Lilly Entwistle, but Neil refused to meet with them then. There had been an interview scheduled to take place at the British Embassy in London, but Neil never showed up and the cops were forced to go home, because they did not have an arrest warrant that could compel Entwistle to talk to them.

It had been more than a month since the murders, and both men were eager to finally set their eyes on the suspect, and put cuffs around the hands they believed had squeezed off the fatal .22-caliber rounds that killed Rachel and Lillian Entwistle. This time they had an arrest warrant that had been issued after an affidavit was filed by another Hopkinton police officer, Sergeant Joseph Bennett, that read:

> On January 22, 2006, the bodies of 27-year-old
> Rachel Entwistle and her 9-month-old daughter
> Lillian were found next to each other in bed in
> their home in Hopkinton, Massachusetts.
> Rachel was last heard from by a friend on the
> evening of January 19, 2006. An autopsy re-
> vealed that Rachel died from a single .22-
> caliber gunshot wound to the head, and Lillian
> died from a single .22-caliber gunshot wound to
> chest (which passed through her body and into
> her mother's left breast). There was no sign of a
> forced entry or break-in to the home, and no
> shell casings were found. The husband and fa-
> ther Neil Entwistle and the family's sole car
> were missing from the premises. The car was lo-
> cated by police in a parking garage at Logan In-
> ternational Airport, Boston, Massachusetts. It
> was locked and unoccupied with the keys inside.
> Airport records revealed that the car entered the
> garage at approximately 10:49 PM on January
> 20, 2006. Airline records show that Neil En-
> twistle purchased a one-way ticket to London,
> England, at approximately 5:00 AM on January
> 21, 2006, and flew out of Logan at approxi-
> mately 8:15 AM without any luggage.
>
> On January 23, 2006, police called Neil En-
> twistle at the home of his parents in Worksop, En-
> gland. Entwistle told police that on January 20,
> 2006, at approximately 9 AM, he had left his

Hopkinton, Massachusetts, home to do an errand. He said his wife and daughter were in bed when he left. He said he returned at approximately 11 AM and found his wife and daughter dead from gunshot wounds. He said he did not call for emergency assistance, but instead covered them up and got a knife to kill himself, but could not go through with it. He said he left the home in the family car and drove to his in-law's home in Carver, Massachusetts, to get a gun from his father-in-law so he could kill himself. He said he could not get into the home so he drove to Logan Airport because he wanted to go home to his parents in England. Police discovered keys to the Carver home locked inside the Entwistle car at the airport. A forensic examination of a .22-caliber revolver (to which Neil Entwistle had access and had previously used, but one which Rachel Entwistle had not previously handled) belonging to Entwistle's father in-law revealed that DNA matching Neil Entwistle was found on the grip of the firearm and DNA matching Rachel Entwistle was found on the muzzle end of the firearm. Further police investigation has revealed that prior to January 20, 2006, Neil Entwistle had accumulated debts in the tens of thousands of dollars, had not been unable [sic] to secure employment since his arrival in the United States the Fall of 2005, and had recently expressed a dissatisfaction with his sex life.

A check with the Criminal History Systems Board reveals that Neil Entwistle has neither a license to carry a firearm or a firearm identification card.

The information contained herein is based upon my review of documents and reports as well as conversations with state and local police officers directly involved in this investigation.

The affidavit was signed "under the pains and penalties of perjury" and dated February 8, 2006. That very day, a judge signed off on an arrest warrant and it was sent to the investigators in place in England. At last, the cops were ready to move.

That moment would finally come for them in a chaotic blaze of drama among the shops and row houses in a sleepy London neighborhood at the Royal Oak Tube station on February 9, 2006.

THE NIGHT BEFORE, NEIL Entwistle had left his parents' home and traveled the 150 miles into London to escape the media that had been camped outside for nearly two weeks. Neil Entwistle bode his time trying to explain away his actions to what few friends he had in England. Those friends would eventually tell investigators that Neil's version of the homicides was dramatically different from what they had seen on the telly about the case. Entwistle told them that after he'd found the bodies, he had driven directly to his mother-in-law's workplace and then "gathered with family back in Carver to mourn the news."

But after some time in Carver, "I began to feel left out," Entwistle told his friends.

"I decided to go home to England," he'd said. "I

wanted to be with my own family. I got off the plane and drove to my parents' house."

Neither of the stories had any basis in truth. Obviously, he had never had any contact with the Matterazzos after the deaths. And when he arrived in London on the evening of January 21, a day before police found Rachel and Lillian, he'd actually rented a car and driven 800 miles around England, spending the night in a hotel room an hour past Worksop, before showing up at his parents' home on January 23. It was that day that Trooper Michael Banks was able to reach Entwistle on the phone and heard the story about Neil finding the bodies after he'd gone out to run some errands.

When Banks asked who would want to kill his family, Neil wept and said, "I don't know."

"We just moved to Hopkinton. No one knows where we live, just a couple of people, friends and family."

Banks asked if he was having any professional problems that would provide the motive for the murders.

"I don't have any problems like that. I did have a job interview that had fallen through. I didn't tell Rachel about it because I think she would have been disappointed. But I have no idea who would do this."

Entwistle had also made phone calls, including one particularly audacious one he'd placed two days before his arrest, to Michael Fee, the attorney representing the owners of the Hopkinton house at 6 Cubs Path.

"This is Neil Entwistle," he'd said calmly into the lawyer's machine, as if he were a simple tenant rather than a suspected double-murderer. "I have no interest in the house anymore. You can send me back the security deposit and last month's rent. I do want to pick up the furniture, and my belongings. This needs to be taken care of in the appropriate manner."

Then there was a pause on the answering machine. It must have hit him how people might judge that kind of phone call—that it could show how cold and callous he really was. Just weeks after his wife and baby had been killed in that house, he was trying to squeeze a couple grand from its owners. Already, the landlords would have a very difficult time renting 6 Cubs Path with the taint of such a horrific crime having occurred there.

"I'll probably leave everything to Rachel's family, Priscilla and Joe Matterazzo. They live in Carver," Neil said before blurting, "But, we need to discuss this."

He then rattled off the international code and phone number to his parents' home.

Of course, Fee immediately called the prosecutor on the case and turned over a recording of the call, which just gave investigators another reason to think that Neil Entwistle was a lowlife coward consumed with greed and eerily unfazed by the deaths of his wife and daughter.

During those days that Neil Entwistle spent on the run in England, members of the press were not the only ones monitoring his every move. Worksop police acknowledged that American investigators had asked them to keep a close eye on him as he stayed with his parents, which they did, from January 31, when he left the house for the first time since driving in Worksop, until the morning of February 9, when London's

Metropolitan Police Extradition Unit, an arm of Scotland Yard, was preparing to close in on him.

Just before 11:45 a.m., the Metropolitan Police asked officials who run the Underground public transportation system to stop a train that they had seen Entwistle board going in the direction of central London a bit earlier. The officers boarded the train, hefted Entwistle to his feet and cuffed his hands behind his back—disappointing the Massachusetts investigators who were hoping to be the ones to put the silver bracelets on. Entwistle didn't put up a fight, but still, the arrest created a scene. Spectators spilled onto the tidy streets and watched as the police pushed the lanky, disheveled man into an awaiting white van and whisked him off.

An insurance broker named Kristian Watlin watched the commotion from his office window and would later explain the scene to a pack of reporters. "I didn't think much of it until I heard shouting." The shouts came from people who, when realizing the suspect was Entwistle, began to hiss and boo at him.

As Entwistle was rushed to a nearby courthouse, other investigators searched his parents' home and their garage, leaving with bins filled with evidence. His parents and his brother, Russell, refused to say a word in Neil's defense as the officers worked. A neighbor watched the cops move in and out of the Entwistle home and heard that their son had been charged. He then muttered under his breath, "Killing your own baby? I hope he gets the death penalty. I'd pull the switch myself."

That same afternoon, Entwistle shuffled into a

brief court hearing at central London's Bow Street magistrates' office wearing baggy gray sweatpants, a black sweatshirt and black sneakers. Alison Riley, an English prosecutor who was acting on behalf of the United States government, only gave very brief details of what the scraggly-looking man in handcuffs was accused of.

"He has committed two murders in America on or before January twenty-first this year," she said.

When she was done speaking, Senior District Judge Timothy Workman turned his attention to the man in front of him and asked, "Do you understand that allegation that you have just heard?"

"Yes I do," Entwistle said, his voice steady.

"I understand you have been asked about the possibility of your consenting about your return to the United States, and I understand that you are choosing not to do so at this time?" Workman said.

"At this stage, yes. I do not want to go back. Not at this time."

For Trooper Banks and Detective vanRaalten, the five-minute hearing was cathartic—the first time it was truly clear that someone would face charges in one of the most chilling murder cases either man had ever investigated. But it was also infuriating. If Entwistle fought extradition it could be months, or even more than a year, before he would be on trial back in the United States. Under English law, a full extradition hearing must be held within two months of the formal request, but even if a judge decided to send Entwistle back to the United States, the suspect could hold up that move with an appeal.

Guilt—or maybe it was fear—apparently set in as Neil Entwistle spent his first-ever night in a jail cell on February 9, 2006. The morning after his arrest, he changed his mind about the extradition process and told British Judge Nicholas Evans that he would be willing to go back to the United States as soon as possible.

"You are aware that your decision is irrevocable?" Evans asked him.

"Yes, sure, whatever," Entwistle replied, before scribbling his name on a waiver.

Hours later, his extradition order was signed.

Entwistle's attorney, Judith Seddon, would explain that her client wanted to "cooperate with the authorities in any way that he can, and he is anxious that a delay may cause his late wife's family, and his own, additional distress . . . He believes he will receive a fair and a proper hearing in the USA of these very serious allegations," she said.

The allegations were spelled out in a four-count complaint that had been signed by the Honorable Robert V. Greco the night before. On the complaint the first count read:

On 01/20/2006 [Neil Entwistle] did assault and beat RACHEL ENTWISTLE with intent to murder such person, and by such assault and beating did kill and murder such person

The second count added:

On 01/20/2006 [Neil Entwistle] did assault and beat LILLIAN ENTWISTLE, with intent to murder

*such person, and by such assault and beating
did kill and murder such person*

The third count, read:

*On 01/20/2006 [Neil Entwistle] did own, pos-
sess or transfer possession of a firearm, rifle,
shotgun or ammunition without complying with
the requirements relating to firearm identification cards.*

The fourth count charged Entwistle with carrying
the firearm.

Back in Massachusetts, Joe Flaherty released a
statement on behalf of the outraged family. The Matterazzos had already filed legal documents in court
pushing to gain hold of Rachel's last worldly belongings as Priscilla was the executor of her daughter's estate. Neil was expected to fight that move, but would
relinquish control of his wife's estate, just as he had
of her body. Still, the move could not assuage the pain
that had imprinted itself on the slain woman's friends
and family. "Rachel and Lilly loved Neil very much.
Neil was a trusted husband and father and it is incom-
prehensible how that love and trust was betrayed in
the ultimate act of violence," Priscilla would say
through Flaherty on the day of Neil Entwistle's arrest.

"We are heartbroken and at a loss to understand
how this could happen."

A short time later, District Attorney Martha Coakley called a press conference to lay out the prosecution's theory on how, and why, the deaths had

happened. The small media room was crammed with local media and swarms of British reporters who had remained in the Boston area. Surrounded by her staff, Coakley reminded the throngs that Entwistle was innocent until proven guilty. The press had grown increasingly impatient with Coakley, though, after she'd asked for the court to seal documents related to the Entwistle arrest—infuriating many reporters who saw her request as a violation of the First Amendment, and knew that if the judge decided to grant her request it would make their jobs that much harder.

"On Thursday night [January 19, 2006], Rachel was alive and had spoken with family members," Coakley said.

"Sometime on Friday morning, Neil Entwistle—with a firearm we believe he had secured at some time before that from father-in-law Joseph Matterazzo—shot Rachel Entwistle in the head and then proceeded to shoot baby Lillian, who was lying on the bed next to her mother.

"We believe possibly this was intended to be a murder–suicide, but we cannot confirm that. Obviously the murder was effected, but the suicide was not.

"What we believe happened next was that Neil Entwistle returned the gun to his father-in-law's home in Carver, then made preparations to leave the country.

"As we know, he was observed at Logan International Airport. He purchased a one-way ticket on British Airways at approximately five a.m. on Saturday morning, January twenty-second. He was on an eight-fifteen flight to the United Kingdom on that day. He was then in Worksop with his parents.

"Based upon forensic information late Tuesday afternoon that linked the .twenty-two handgun owned by Joseph Matterazzo both to Neil Entwistle and to Rachel, we believed we had probable cause to seek an arrest warrant for Neil Entwistle's arrest."

The swift arrest of a high-profile suspect so quickly after the slaying was a coup for Martha Coakley, especially when compared with the success rate of the Boston Police Department, which had been recently assailed as having the worst homicide clearance rate in the entire country—meaning that most of the killers in the seventy-five murders recorded on the streets of Boston the year before were still out on the streets. It could not be better timing for Coakley, who would launch a bid to become the state's attorney general not long after Neil Entwistle was cuffed. The arrest bolstered her image as a no-nonsense, get-action law woman.

On the day Entwistle was arrested in Britain, Coakley took advantage of the intense media scrutiny to beef up her profile by appearing on CNN with Anderson Cooper. Cooper asked her about her statement that the crime was an apparent murder-suicide attempt, and, as Neil Entwistle had clearly not killed himself, what she was basing her theory on.

"Of course, when you look at domestic violence profile cases, you know, if something happens in the heat of passion, and it's unplanned, you would have more evidence of a fight, a crime scene. If it was something that had been planned, but the perpetrator wanted to get away, it would probably be planned better . . .

"But the idea that he planned to do this because of

financial situations or because he was overwhelmed is—is really one of the theories that makes sense, under the circumstances," Coakley said, her red close-cropped hair stylishly gelled on her forehead.

Cooper asked her if there had been any attempt by the killer to clean up the crime scene, and Coakley said no, bolstering her theory that it was a crime of passion, not a hired hit, as the British press had been suggesting.

Besides, Coakley said, it appeared that Rachel had not been aware "until fairly recently" that the family was in such a dire financial state.

Cooper said that the perople he'd spoken with who knew Neil all described him as being "a lovely guy," who "couldn't have been nicer."

"And that's, I think, part of what makes this, in some ways, so sad and somewhat inexplicable," Coakley replied. ". . . He's the totally unlikely defendant. There was nothing that might have indicated that this is the way this young marriage, this young family would have turned out. And that is what makes it so sad."

CHAPTER 13

ON VALENTINE'S DAY IN 2006—a holiday that Rachel Entwistle had always appreciated because it symbolized love and happiness and romance, all of the things that she'd felt like she had finally achieved in her marriage—her husband, was whisked aboard an airplane in England and flown back to Massachusetts to be formally arraigned on charges that he had murdered his wife and daughter.

He had left London's Gatwick Airport on a commercial flight early that morning with shackles around his swollen ankles and his hands cuffed to a full-body harness locked by the armed marshals. Among the guards was William Fallon, chief deputy of the US Marshals in Massachusetts at the time. No one was taking any chances in this case, even if it was true that the suspect hardly looked dangerous while wearing white socks that were squeezed tight between his big toes by the pair of plastic flip-flops he had been issued.

Once the flight landed in Bangor, Maine, Entwistle was met at the airport by another phalanx of state troopers who helped marshals escort him onto a private government plane dubbed "Con Air" by law enforcement types. Con Air, used to move high-risk prisoners, Mafia cooperators and the country's most vicious and dangerous convicts to maximum-security prisons, is a sleek jet with the words "UNITED STATES OF AMERICA" emblazoned across the side. It dropped out of the clouds and landed among a glare of police lights and a crush of television cameras all angling for the perfect shot of the accused killer. As the plane came to a stop on the tarmac at tiny Hanscom Airfield just northwest of Boston, reporters began to jostle each other. There was even some shoving, as the doors flung up and marshals and state troopers began to escort the shackled man off the plane. After a transatlantic drama that had captivated two nations for more than a month now, Neil Entwistle was finally back in Massachusetts to face charges in connection with what investigators believe was an insidious burst of violence prompted by mounting debt and the desire for "a fit more fun in the bedroom."

Moving slowly because of the full-body shackles that encased his body, Entwistle was prodded into the Hopkinton Police Department, where Detective vanRaalten would roll Entwistle's fingertips over an ink pad and then press them to a booking sheet. A mug shot was taken, which Neil actually smiled for, a little bit. After Entwistle was processed on the double-homicide charge, he was then pushed into a six-foot-by-ten-foot cell in the police station. He would spend the night there and then be transported in handcuffs and shackles to his arraignment at Framingham District

Court the following day. It would be the first time in the department's history that an accused killer would spend the night the concrete slab and thin cotton mattress that served as the jail's bed. The cell, with its stainless-steel sink, a toilet and a concrete slab with a couple of scratchy blankets for a cot, was a far cry from the luxury that Entwistle had just months before acquired—albeit on credit.

Within seconds of Entwistle arriving on U.S. soil, bloggers were trading details of his transport to the Hopkinton jail cell, and cyber sleuths were coming up with their own theories of the case online. It was ironic that Entwistle would be such a macabre online celebrity: it was the Internet that had sunk him into such colossal debt—and would provide prosecutors with much of the evidence used to obtain an arrest warrant to charge him.

The blogosphere was alive with ramblings and websites chronicling the Entwistle case. Computer mavens dubbed the murders of Rachel and Lillian Entwistle the first-ever homicide case that would allow investigators to utilize the "WHOIS.com" database—a high-tech program that tracks website owners. Within minutes of the murders, true-crime blogs were full of information on Entwistle's sordid sex sites and Internet get-rich-quick schemes. Rachel Morgan, who ran RLM & Associates—described as an *America's Most Wanted* sort of web service that posts sites to try to find missing children and generate tips in high-profile criminal cases—bought and registered the domain www.neilentwistle.com. "He does not have ownership of that and he will never gain ownership of that," Morgan told a reporter. "We represent the victims 100 percent. If Neil could have gotten a hold of [the site name], he could have profited from it and we did not want that to happen."

Obviously, the case prosecutors planned to present against Neil Entwistle was not just about what he'd had on his mind at the time of the murders, but also what was on his computer. And for someone who boasted of his computer prowess, Entwistle did not have the good sense that an average teenager peeking at porn or other illicit materials would have to erase the history listing his favorite columns. He did not wipe out the frightening Web searches for killings and suicide and euthanasia that he had conducted just days before the slayings. He didn't even try to hide his search for whores on websites like Eye Candy Entertainment, or his ownership of a bevy of questionable get-rich ventures.

One popular site, www.huffcrimeblog.com immediately began to scour databases for background on Entwistle as readers began to trade online theories like these:

Neil Entwistle . . . Pimpin'
    . . . Neil Entwistle, the 27-year-old Briton now accused of murdering his wife Rachel and their infant daughter Lillian on January 20, 2006, in Hopkinton, MA. Mike left, as readers of this blog have thankfully done numerous times lately, a very interesting link.
    Certainly one of the first things I did upon seeing www.srpublications.co.uk linked to Entwistle

The Entwistle family—Neil, Rachel and baby Lillian Rose—in happier times.

Courtesy of *Boston Herald*

Mommy Rachel with Lillian Rose.

Courtesy of *Boston Herald*

Lillian Rose with the smile that would melt her grandparents' hearts.

Courtesy of *Boston Herald*

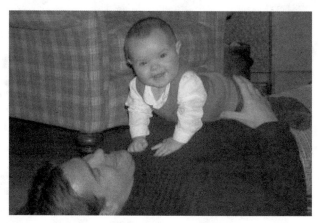

Neil snuggles with Lillian Rose.

Courtesy of *Boston Herald*

Neil's parents, Clifford and Yvonne Entwistle, with their grand-daughter, Lillian Rose.

Courtesy of the family

Baby Lillian Rose is christened in Plymouth, Massachusetts.

Courtesy of *Boston Herald*

Former Massachusetts State Trooper Joseph Flaherty, the spokesman for Priscilla and Joseph Matterazzo after Rachel and Lillian Rose were found dead in their bedroom.

Courtesy of *Boston Herald*

Neil outside his parents' home in Worksop, England. He is still wearing his wedding ring, which was taken from him after his arrest.

Courtesy of *Boston Herald*

Sally, the basset hound that was left alone in a crate when Neil Entwistle fled Massachusetts for England.

Courtesy of *Boston Herald*

Priscilla and Joe Matterazzo at the gravesite of Rachel and Lillian Rose in Massachusetts.

Courtesy of *Boston Herald*

Eben Howard, the man accused of kicking Neil Entwistle in the stomach in the Cambridge jail house.

Courtesy of *Boston Herald*

Middlesex Assistant District Attorney Michael Fabbri.

Courtesy of *Boston Herald*

Rachel's mother, Priscilla Matterazzo, comes into Framingham District Court with a flower in memory of her slain daughter and granddaughter on February 16, 2006, after Entwistle's arrest in England.

Courtesy of *Boston Herald*

Neil, flanked by Hopkinton Police Detectives Scott vanRaalten and John Porter, and wearing a bulletproof vest, his hands and feet shackled as he walks into Framingham District Court for his arraignment on murder charges in the deaths of his wife and daughter.

Courtesy of *Boston Herald*

Neil being escorted into Cambridge court in an orange Middlesex County jail jumpsuit, where he is formally charged with murder.

Courtesy of *Boston Herald*

Elliot Weinstein, Neil Entwistle's defense.

Courtesy of *Boston Herald*

Neil as he hears the charges leveled against him in connection with the murders of his wife and baby in their Hopkinton, Massachusetts, home.

Courtesy of *Boston Herald*

Joe Matterazzo clutches his wife Priscilla's hand as Neil Entwistle walks into the courtoom. Priscilla is wearing a tiny silk rose in memory of her granddaughter. The packed courtroom stared at the accused killer.

Courtesy of *Boston Herald*

Neil Entwistle looks away from the packed courtroom.

Courtesy of *Boston Herald*

was check the **_registration (whois) info_** on the domain.

Next thing I did was look it up via **_The Way-back Machine._**

But Mike took a closer look. Specifically at the **_record made of the website on May 31, 2003._** You should know before you click that link that there is a nude photo of a young woman on the page, so consider yourself warned.

What is more interesting in reference to Neil Entwistle, listed as the registrant of srpublica-tions.co.uk beginning in September of 2002, is the text accompanying the nude photo:

> **- FREE UK SEX - FREE UK SEX - FREE UK SEX - FREE UK SEX -**
> We are setting up a **Discrete [sic] UK Sex Contacts** network. To get the service up and running we are offering completely **free membership** to all who are interested. In addition, once the service has a large number of subscribers, you will be eliga-ble [sic] for a generous discount on any fees . . .

It appears he set up a separate e-mail address for this pursuit—freeContactInfo@srpublications. co.uk. The main page for **_all archived versions of the site_** shows that some of the dates have as-terisks (*) beside them—that denotes a change made in the site. It appears that the site was **_changed again on December 5, 2003,_** and I can *only guess that at that time the "Discrete Sex Contacts" advertisement was removed. At that time, it seems as if Entwistle must have decided to focus on marketing "__The Big Penis Manual__," as it is then referred to as their "flagship product."*

This May, 2003 version of Entwistle's srpublications.co.uk page is perhaps only significant in how it might relate to the portion of this story that has apparently been most startling to anyone following developments lately . . . that aside from being in a financial crisis, Neil Entwistle supposedly stated prior to his arrest that there were perhaps sexual issues in his relationship with Rachel.

To me, it seemed that we were perhaps seeing the first hints of the real problem, if Entwistle did kill his wife and child. A pathological narcissist, a psychopath, would be quite accomplished at masking his less savory behaviors by his twenties, if he was of above-average intelligence. But the pressures of supporting a family combined with a lack of gratification physically would quickly produce cracks in that mask. As would moving to a new country, far from the usual support systems.

And I also feel that the slant of these websites tells something about the self Neil was perhaps keeping secret from many people all along. I was struck by the constant appeal to the most base needs . . . it indicated to me that the person behind the site felt that was the quickest way to earn easy money because perhaps such things, particularly the porn, might be appealing to them, as well.

The reason the story of Neil Entwistle allegedly murdering his wife and child has gripped so many people is because it speaks again to the difference between appearances and truth. Rachel's "Knight" was really a porn webmaster who even tried to get a service for swingers off the ground . . . perhaps even an escort service, though it is hard to tell from the "discrete" blurb quoted above. It doesn't mean Neil was one (a swinger), himself, but it does show where his head was a good deal of the time.

I wonder how well a lovely wife and beautiful baby girl ever truly fit into the picture such a man had of his life . . . if they ever did, at all. It would have been mighty hard to hook swingers up for free if you spent the rest of your time fashioning the facade of "the happy family."

Sex was probably the last thing on Neil Entwistle's mind on February 15, 2006, as he laid his head on the hard concrete of the Hopkinton jail cot, pulled a harsh wool blanket up to his chin, and tried desperately with a few minutes of sleep in a cold, dark cell, to blot out the nightmare his life had become.

CHAPTER 14

A CROWD HAD SLOWLY begun to ooze out of the public housing development outside of Framingham District Court as a motorcade of ten cars with pulsing lights and sirens caused an unexpected surge of excitement in the sleepy industrial area. It was all part of the process necessary to convey Neil Entwistle to his arraignment. The convoy had the aspect of a Secret Service transport for the president of the United States of America rather than protection for a British expatriate accused of a grisly crime, and now being pilloried on talk radio shows and blasted by columnists around the globe. It was all very riveting to the residents of the projects on Pearl Harbor Road, who were all too used to the drone of police sirens, though never at this sort of magnitude. Add to that the panoply of satellite media trucks that wrapped thick cables around what seemed like the entire circumference of the two-story, red-brick courthouse, and the perfectly coiffed TV reporters who stood underneath the towering antennas chatting like a pack of pigeons, answering their chirping Nextels and updating each other with ETAs from their counterparts flying in four helicopters overhead as the motorcade made its way to the courthouse. There were more than 200 reporters vying for a glimpse of the accused murderer.

To add even more intrigue, the caravan passed a hand-scrawled sign attached to a telephone pole that read:

ENTWISTLE, YOU'RE A DEAD MAN.

The drama was ratcheted up even more when police pulled Neil Entwistle out of a Massachusetts State Police car. Cameramen crowded the cruiser like a swarm of angry bees when it passed by, slowing it to a near stop. Neil was in the back seat with a seatbelt strapped across his lumpy body and his head facing away from the incessant flash of camera bulbs and the intense glow of TV lights.

Entwistle was flanked by Hopkinton Detective Scott vanRaalten and Hopkinton Detective John Porter. Both men were in plainclothes and vanRaalten had his badge around his neck on a chain. Both men had on sensible shoes and black leather jackets that accentuated their muscular frames. They looked beefy next to Neil Entwistle, who was clearly soft, despite his height. A black bulletproof vest ran from his shoulders to his lower abdomen, and his hands were shackled to chains around his waist.

One woman who had emerged from the projects to watch, clutched a yapping Chihuahua to her chest and began to screech as the motorcade passed.

"Murderer! Murderer!" Maria Quinones was quoted as screaming in the papers the following morning.

"Burn in hell!" she yelled as Entwistle was ushered past the cacophony of sirens and TV cameras and blue kleigs set up outside—so many lights that, from a distance, it might have appeared to be a summer-time carnival.

"You sick animal!" yelled another neighbor. "You suck!"

Angelica Carrillo, another rubbernecker outside the courthouse, tried to quiet her.

"The man needs help," he drawled in a thick Hispanic accent with hints of a Boston twang. "That's all. He needs help."

Clad in a gray sweat suit, a black fleece top and flip-flops, Entwistle faced the judge, but refused to make eye contact with Rachel's family. His eyes darted nervously around the room, as if he were un-sure where to fix his gaze. A photograph would cap-ture him looking maniacal, his pupils pushed to the right corner of his eyes and his thin lips pulled into a tight scowl. A single strand of brown hair flapped on his forehead.

For that second, immortalized with a digital image, Neil Entwistle looked like a man possessed by the Devil.

Joe and Priscilla Matterazzo could not believe they were so close to Neil, who just weeks earlier had stood in their kitchen with his arm around Rachel, their baby cradled in her mother's arms. Loved ones filled the front two rows of the hard wooden pews that faced the back of the defense and prosecution tables. Each of the women there to support Priscilla Matterazzo held a bouquet of orange daylilies, baby's breath and a single pink rose, in memory of Rachel and Lillian. Neil steadfastly pretended not to notice the flowers. Or his in-laws. Or the friends who now glared at him, secretly embarrassed that they had worked so hard to make him feel welcome when he moved to Massachusetts.

No matter how deep the shock of his circumstances had set in, it was impossible for Neil not to notice the phalanx of police officers crammed into the courthouse: "thirty deputy sheriffs, eleven trial court officers, and an untold number of armed state, Hopkinton and Framingham police enveloped the court with a blue curtain of security that was declared extraordinary," the *Boston Herald*'s court reporter Laurel J. Sweet would write. Sweet, a stunning blonde scribe who had been featured in a documentary running at full speed in four-inch heels, would cover the case from the time the bodies were found on that icy January day.

Even Michael Fabbri, the prosecutor appearing in court on behalf of the Office of the Middlesex District Attorney, was screened twice by metal detectors before he was allowed to go inside. No one wanted to take any chances that the proceedings would be interrupted by a maniac hell-bent on his own brand of justice for the murdered mother and child.

"Priscilla and Joseph Matterazzo had just four minutes to study their son-in-law's face for answers to their unanswerable questions," Sweet wrote. "Priscilla

Matterazzo . . . stared numbly at Entwistle, but never succeeded in catching his eye."

Just as he had weeks earlier at the funeral, Joe Matterazzo, wearing a black leather jacket that made him appear imposing, looked ashen and just sat silently with his hand firmly gripping his wife's, his own knuckles getting white as he heard the charges read aloud by a stranger:

"Murder in the first degree: Rachel Entwistle.

"Murder in the first degree: Lillian Entwistle.

"Illegal possession of a firearm.

"Illegal possession of ammunition."

Entwistle did not say a single word. His face was stony as his attorney, Elliot Weinstein, entered a plea of not guilty. Judge Robert Greco ordered the accused killer held without bail. Weinstein did not protest his client's bail status. Greco had a state psychiatrist on call for the day just in case a psychiatric evaluation was ordered, but Neil Entwistle's mental state was never called into question.

And in just four minutes, the hearing was over.

But the pain for those affected by the killings would continue for a very, very long time to come.

"Seeing Neil Entwistle standing accused of this awful crime gives us little comfort and, in fact, only adds to our enormous pain and suffering. To think that someone we loved, trusted, opened our home to could do this to our daughter and granddaughter is beyond belief," Priscilla and Joe Matterazzo would announce in a statement read by their longtime friend Joe Flaherty, who had been by the family's side and acted as their spokesman since the murder. The friends and family who had crammed the courthouse stood around the Matterazzos holding hands as Flaherty read the statement. Some cried as Flaherty spoke—his state police training keeping his voice steady. Even the utter disgust he felt at seeing Neil Entwistle's pale, puffy face did not affect Flaherty's demeanor.

"The betrayal to this family, to Neil's family, to our family, to our friends here and in the UK is unbearable. From what we have learned through the course of the investigation, we are only now coming to realize the level of his deceit.

"We are astonished and devastated to learn of the hidden life of Neil Entwistle. We never suspected that Neil was anything other than a loving father, a trusted son-in-law and a husband. Neil betrayed our trust in so many different ways that it is almost impossible to describe it.

"What is most outrageous in our eyes is that he entered our home twice during the course of these crimes—once to take the murder weapon and arm himself, and a second time . . . to hide the weapon," Flaherty said, using the word "murder" even though the charges against Neil Entwistle had not been proven. The words seemed unreal even to him.

But he went on.

"We also want to thank all the people from the United States and England who have sent hundreds of cards with their support, their love and their prayers. [They] are a great comfort to us during this time."

Outside the courthouse, Weinstein—a swaggering attorney who preferred spit-shined cowboy boots to high-end Newbury Street loafers—argued that the un-mitigated media coverage of the slayings would make it extremely difficult to defend his client.

"I don't know that Mr. Entwistle will ever be able to get a fair trial on these charges," Weinstein told the throng of reporters outside on the courthouse steps. "I am certain that anybody watching this telecast [the four-minute proceeding had been streamed live over the networks], or reading the reporting of today's ar-raignment, has already formed an opinion with re-spect to Mr. Entwistle's guilt.

"There should not be a case, ever, where the media does nothing but stage an event to the detriment of the accused's opportunity to a fair trial," Weinstein said. Then, he sat on the courthouse steps, crossed a booted foot over one leg of his tailored suit, and posed for a still photographer with his hands gripping his knee. The sun shone off his bald head, making him seem even paler than he had inside under the harsh fluores-cent lights. Sunglasses gave him a ghoulish look as a wide grin showed his perfectly straight, Crest Whitestripped teeth.

It seemed more like some sort of scripted specta-cle than a court appearance for an alleged killer. The fascination went far beyond the reach of newspapers and television, though. On dozens of websites, the Neil Entwistle "event" was updated by the second across sites like www.websleuths.com:

The fascination with the case spanned the globe, and the Internet helped fuel armchair crime buffs who spent hours exchanging small details in the case and their own theories. It was a relatively new phenomenon in the United States, one that had begun as the police chased O.J. Simpson's SUV through Los Angeles, an image that was streamed across computer screens in every corner of the country, and escalated with such cases as Louise Woodward's, Scott Peterson's, and now Neil Entwistle's.

Back in England, Cliff and Yvonne Entwistle took in their son's hearing by watching television in their own home. In fact, they may have been among the only people on the planet who, as their son's attorney predicted, had "already formed an opinion with respect to Mr. Entwistle's guilt."

"Our son is one hundred percent innocent," Yvonne Entwistle would snap to a reporter, her voice as clipped and controlled as it was when she would call to her boys to come in from the back garden.

Her husband, ever the politician, was a bit more diplomatic. "People are being very kind to us, and realize what a difficult situation we are in," he told a British reporter. "They sympathize with the family situation, and sympathize with our great loss."

The Matterazzos were not interested in sharing the Entwistles' grief. The two sets of grandparents had not spoken since the days after the bodies were found.

Priscilla Matterazzo, still clutching her ribbon-wrapped bouquet, was escorted to her own car. She wore a short brown leather coat with a fur collar, and hid her tears behind small round-framed sunglasses. A young court officer placed a hand on the small of her shoulder, a gesture that seemed to say, *I can't imagine what you are going through.* Even the hardened reporters who had covered dozens of heinous crimes—some even worse than the one described in court that afternoon—sucked in a breath to contain their own tears from rushing up unexpectedly when confronted by the devastation that the murders had caused.

In all likelihood, both the Matterazzos and the Entwistles watched the television footage at some point on February 16, 2006, of Neil being escorted out a back door of the Massachusetts courthouse wearing an orange jumpsuit with the words MIDDLESEX JAIL INMATE emblazoned on the front and back, and government-issued sneakers, the all-white canvas kind that some mothers used to buy in the bargain bin at a supermarket.

A uniformed state trooper brought him outside, both arms wrapped around Neil's elbow, his gait slowed by the shackles around his ankles. He was placed back in a police cruiser for the twenty-minute ride to the Middlesex jail on Thorndike Street in Cambridge, Massachusetts, located in a concrete high-rise that contains the criminal courthouse on the lower floors. The transport van drove into a secure garage, and then pulled into an elevator where Entwistle was taken to the twentieth floor of the building. The deputy sheriffs charged with protecting Entwistle from harm in jail were already abuzz, using law enforcement parlance in their whispers about the new inmate, that he was a "P.O.S."—Piece of Shit—if he had committed the terrible crime he was accused of.

Before he was escorted to his new digs, which he would not see the outside of for a very long time, Entwistle was showered, fingerprinted and given a set of jailhouse scrubs to change into. The sweats and black shirt he had worn to his court appearance that day were tagged with his name and stuffed into a storeroom.

It came as little surprise to anyone in the jail system that Middlesex Sheriff James DiPaola assigned Neil Entwistle to a private cell in the medical unit. It measured eight feet by six feet, ringed by bars with a narrow bed, a sink, a toilet and a small bookshelf that held a Bible. In fact, it was smaller than any of the three bathrooms in the posh 2,432–square-foot house in Hopkinton that he had fled from less than a month before. Entwistle was being held in the medical unit primarily because the sheriff considered him a suicide risk, and routinely, anyone suspected of being a threat to himself is housed where staff can monitor him with visual images beamed from inside. Entwistle would not be allowed to intermingle with other inmates and would have his food delivered to him on a tray in his cell. It was all part of the process of keeping him alive so he could face the charges that had been brought against him.

Neil Entwistle was not the only killer who'd spent time in that room. There was Michael "Mucko" Mc-Dermott, the software technology tester who got up from his desk at Edgewater Technology in the small town of Wakefield, Massachusetts, on December 26, 2000, and, using three different assault weapons, gunned down seven of his colleagues. Several of those killed were processing garnishment of his wages pursuant to an Internal Revenue Service levy for $5,586 in back taxes. McDermott's attorneys argued that he was insane, but a jury found him guilty and he is currently serving seven life sentences—one for each victim.

McDermott's case was streamed live on Court TV, as was the trial of two child killers, Salvatore Sicari and Charles Jaynes, who had spent months in the Middlesex Jail's medical unit where Entwistle was now. The two men were convicted of kidnapping and drugging their neighbor's 10-year-old son, Jeffrey Curley, in 1997, and then raping the boy's dead body after strangling him to death. In their case, being housed in the medical unit was for their protection from other inmates, not themselves, as they were not just pedophiles, their legal bills were being paid in part by members of the controversial North American Man Boy Love Association, which encouraged sex between children and adults, and it was all too likely that they would be murdered by angry cons.

So the deputy sheriffs who would be watching Entwistle's every move were long since accustomed to dealing with the worst of the worst. What they were unprepared for was how nonchalantly Entwistle handled the dramatic change to his lifestyle.

"I find it extremely interesting how calm he is, sort of matter-of-fact about what he's going through," Di-Paola told the *Boston Herald* shortly after Entwistle was incarcerated. "He's very even-keeled. He moves very slowly. He lost some weight, but he said that was okay, that he was probably a little overweight and needed to lose some weight.

"It's an extremely isolated existence," DiPaola said. "For one hour a day he can exercise or shower. If he tells us he wants a change, then we change it. He was seeing our psychologist for a while, but said he didn't want to see him anymore."

Even when Superior Court Justice Peter Lauriat ordered that he provide a DNA swab—"as minimal a sample as necessary," on the very off chance that the DNA extrapolated from the Dasani bottle in the BMW at Logan Airport was not his—Neil calmly opened his mouth and let a forensic investigator run a buccal stick across the inside of his cheek. After it was slipped into an evidence bag and carefully marked, the sample was shipped to the State Police Crime Laboratory in Sudbury, Massachusetts.

Entwistle would have no visitors and would spend his time reading the Bible. It was an appropriate choice: God seemed to be the only entity Neil Entwistle could rely upon as prosecutors continued to build what appeared to be a rock-solid case against him. One guard who had delivered stacks of hate mail addressed to Neil Entwistle from all over the world said, "The level of hatred felt about this guy is terrifying."

CHAPTER 15

"YOU ARE A DESPICABLE human being and a scum-bag," the voice on the other end of the line growled at Eric Weinstein after waking him up on the morning side of midnight one day in March 2006.

"How's it feel to help a baby killer?" a caller who left a message on his office phone asked. "Maybe someone should put a bullet in your head," another said.

The only problem was, the callers were threatening and haranguing the wrong attorney with the last name Weinstein. The Boston lawyer they were looking for was Elliot Weinstein. The one-time president of the Massachusetts Association of Criminal Defense Lawyers, Weinstein felt strongly that attorneys should always mount a strong defense, no matter how grue-some the crime their client is accused of. He also felt that defense attorneys assigned to a case by the court, and not hired by deep-pocketed clients, should show the same zeal earning taxpayers' money as they would charging more from someone whose gains may have been ill-gotten. He would often remark that "everyone's entitled to a defense. Everyone's entitled to a presumption of innocence."

So, those phone threats would not have bothered him—he was accustomed to being attacked for the type of clients that he represented.

Over the years Weinstein had accrued an impressive client list that included some of the state's most notorious rogues: mobsters and murderers, gang bangers and sexual deviants, sadistic rapists and kid killers, crack dealers and gun sellers. There was no perpetrator too tainted for Weinstein, no suspect undeserving of the best defense representation available.

At least two of his cases had involved gang leaders, street thugs prosecuted for flooding cities all over Massachusetts with weapons. One of his clients was the reputed leader of the Latin Kings gang, Paul "King Ghost" Follis, who was facing federal cocaine and weapons charges. Another was Gordon Robinson, a reputed crack dealer and leader of the Intervale Posse street gang, that had seized control of entire corners in Roxbury and Mattapan, the Boston neighborhoods historically hardest hit by gun violence. In the late 1990s, during the height of the crack epidemic in Boston, Robinson was one of fifteen gang bangers rousted in a sweep. An indictment named him as a shooter in the assault of a man who'd survived a gun blast to the face. As part of the defense, Weinstein ripped apart cooperators who would testify against his client. "They've received favorable treatment," he said in court during the trial. Days later, Robinson would be one of the gang members who created a melee in the federal lockup where he was being held, hurling death threats and feces at corrections officers. Law enforcement officials had a special disdain for the Intervale Posse because members of the gang had boasted of killing a prosecutor named Paul McLaughlin, who was stalked and executed in the parking lot of a commuter line train station in a Boston neighborhood. During the ruckus at the prison, a corrections officer told authorities that one of the Intervale Posse men had screeched, "Yeah, we'll get them like the one we got by the railroad," as another chimed in, "Yeah, we'll do this DA just like the one by the tracks." Weinstein would tell a reporter that the taunts made behind the wall were "the comments of men confined all day in a jail cell."

Weinstein also represented a Charlestown man who'd opened fire on a recovering drug addict named Albert "Albie" Titcomb in the hallway of a housing project over a $50 cocaine debt in 1994. People in Charlestown—a neighborhood nationally famous for proliferation of bank robbers and the "code of silence" that kids in the neighborhood grow up adhering to, making it difficult to solve cases with no cooperators—were so outraged over Titcomb's death, police were actually able to arrest the killer, Shaun Fritz, Weinstein's client, and prosecutors were able to convict him. Titcomb's mom, Terry, would go on to create "Mothers Against Murder"—a program that would sadly help hundreds of parents deal with the violent deaths of their loved ones.

By no means was Neil Entwistle the first accused baby killer Weinstein had defended, and he had already unsuccessfully tried to keep several men accused of

killing their wives in grisly murders out of prison.
Juan Cruz had beaten 6-year-old Eric Dawood to
death after the child had wet himself while sitting on
Cruz's lap. Cruz, a convicted bank robber, had refused to bring him to the hospital and only after a
neighbor called 911 did the boy get help. Prosecutors
said the little boy had broken ribs, torn intestines, and
bruises that covered the entire span of his tiny body.
In a stunning reversal, Cruz's conviction was later vacated on a technicality. Vao Sok was convicted of
snatching his neighbor's 6-year-old daughter and
dragging her into an abandoned building, where he
raped and suffocated her and left her to die alone in a
1992 attack. Weinstein's argument that Sok had been
traumatized by his experiences in Cambodia's killing
fields, and did not have the intelligence to pull off
such a dastardly crime failed to convince the jury,
who sent Sok to prison for life. In the same year that
Sok killed the little girl, Weinstein defended William
Zagrodny, who had murdered his wife, Karla, in their
Massachusetts home by stomping on her and then
strangling her to death. He is serving life behind bars.

One of the most gruesome murders in Massachusetts history came at the hands of another one of
Weinstein's clients, Joseph Romano, who would be
convicted of killing and dismembering his wife,
Katherine Leonard Romano. The young mother's body
was never found and she was identified only by DNA
found in brain matter recovered from a neighbor's
handsaw. After the 2000 trial, Romano told a judge that
Weinstein was more interested in garnering publicity
for his law practice than providing fair representation.

Romano even claimed that Weinstein had told him the outcome didn't matter because the case was "good for business." Weinstein steadfastly denied that, telling the judge, "I would never put forward less effort because a person is indigent. I couldn't give a damn about publicity—good or bad."

But for a guy who didn't give a damn about publicity, Weinstein managed to put himself in the middle of plenty of high-profile cases. In 2005, twins Peter and Daniel McGuane of Ayer, Massachusetts, were arrested on charges that they had beaten 19-year-old Kelly Proctor to death as he walked home from the town's fireworks display with his girlfriend. The victim had desperately scrambled under a car to avoid the twins' blows, but the wounds that had already been delivered with shod feet and balled fists were fatal, and the twins were arrested on manslaughter charges. They turned right to Elliot Weinstein to represent them at their arraignment. The McGuane boys had a reputation for being brutal, and had long been nicknamed "the Evil Twins" in the small town. Just years before, they had been arrested for beating each other up—with cleats on their feet—and Peter had been charged with assaulting his own mother during that same fight. As part of the defense strategy, Weinstein attempted to blame the McGuanes' alleged victim, saying, "He made the initial assault and then and only then did either brother do anything at all. . . . It's clear from what we've learned, there is a lot of misinformation, there's a lot of anger . . . We know that that is going to filter out to the benefit and to the favor of both of the McGuane brothers.

"We know that people in this community, for whatever reason, don't like them," Weinstein told reporters. "But [Proctor] was the major aggressor here."

However, it would be hard for the attorney to explain why two hulking 21-year-old men—the brothers were listed as six-foot-three and six-foot-four, weighing 195 pounds each on their police booking sheets—picked on such a slight victim. Proctor was a star athlete, but stood just five-foot-six and weighed only about 160 pounds. By the time the case finally went to trial in May of 2007, Weinstein had already been replaced by a new defense team, so he would never have to explain those circumstances to a jury. When that day did come in 2007, the jury would find the twins guilty of involuntary manslaughter and sentence each of them to just five years in prison. The twins have vowed to appeal that meager sentence.

Then there was the guard at Deer Island prison who was convicted of forcing a woman to have sex with other men, attacks that he captured on videotape and dispersed. The guard, James M. Bowen, pleaded guilty and was sentenced to eight years in prison despite his assertions to a judge that he "didn't trust" his attorney, Elliot Weinstein. That case came after Weinstein represented a burglar charged with murdering a man during the commission of a home invasion. His client was accused of dangling the naked victim out a second-story window before dropping him to his death.

Each one of the cases that Weinstein became involved in had enough sex, violence and bloodshed to satisfy the gore-hungry media, and practically guarantee him front-page positioning. One case in particular turned into a virtual media circus when he defended Ismael Vasquez, one of four people in a rag-tag gang charged with the kidnapping, rape and murder of a homeless drifter named Io Nachtwey.

Nachtwey, a bright, promising 22-year-old runaway from Hawaii who spoke four languages, had befriended her killers after meeting them in the famed Harvard Square "Pit," where homeless outcasts would gather to panhandle for change, smoke butts, skateboard and pickpocket commuters leaving the subway. Ismael Vasquez was in charge of enticing newcomers into the gang, which they called an outpost of the Crips. Weinstein's client, like the other posturing suburban kids who formed the so-called gang, carried on as if they really were in a violent criminal enterprise. They even held a swearing-in ceremony for new prospects in a cemetery, after which gang initiates were taught to wield knives and guns, and to commit robberies—always cautioned that they must make sure to intimidate victims into giving up their PIN numbers when they stole ATM cards.

Soon, the inevitable happened when social misfits are asked to undertake violent gang missions: the requests became too violent even for the willing volunteers. One girl in the crew was told to slit the throat of another who had "disrespected the Crips' colors." She ran back to her parents' home in a posh town far from the Pit in Cambridge.

The gang had those kind of blood-thirsty overtones when in 2001, Vasquez, his brother and two others lured Nachtwey to a remote railroad bridge, where she was raped and butchered before her "friends" threw her body into the Charles River.

It was State Trooper Joe Flaherty, the same investigator who was acting as the spokesman for Rachel and Lillian Entwistle's loved ones, who'd responded when her body floated up to the surface near Boston University where it was found by joggers. By then, he had been in charge of the Suffolk County District Attorney's Office detectives for two years, and had more than a decade of homicide experience before that.

Initially, it was thought that Nachtwey was a suicide, a "floater" as they are called by cops. But she had these strange markings on her that one detective thought might have been made by a boat propeller after she'd died. But Flaherty thought otherwise once he saw her small, scarred body in the "southern mortuary," which was what cops called the Suffolk County Medical Examiner's Office.

"Those aren't propeller marks. They're stab wounds," Flaherty said after examining her body. He then pulled on a pair of plastic gloves and moved his meaty hand over the corpse's small, balled-up fingers and slowly, carefully unwound the tight clutch.

There were slices in her palms and on the tips of her fingers. "Defensive wounds," Flaherty remarked. "This is not a floater. This is a homicide."

Days later, Flaherty got a heads-up from the Cambridge police that they had picked up some young "skels"—another cop word for *dirt bag*—in the Pit after they had attempted to abduct someone. A witness jotted down the would-be kidnappers' license plate. One of them, Scott Davenport, was jabbering about a murder, and wanted to cooperate with investigators in exchange for immunity on the kidnapping charge.

Flaherty met with him at the Dedham House of Correction, where he had been separated from his pals, and Davenport told him a story about how Nachtwey had been held down and stabbed while he stood off to the side, "too afraid to run, too afraid to call the police."

His eyes moved to the left or the right when his account fluctuated, his brow furrowed when he talked about his own fear. He stammered over key elements of his story. Flaherty had been a cop long enough to recognize the lies as they came out of Davenport's mouth. As Flaherty prepared to leave the lockup's interview room, he turned back and yelled over his shoulder, "Homicide investigations are about science. If you are lying to me, we are going to find out."

Davenport sat silently, contemplating, but didn't open his mouth.

Flaherty called the State Police Crime Lab and asked them to test the clothes Davenport was wearing the night he was locked up. Every item of clothing was splattered with blood. His sneaker was so soaked through with blood that it had stained his sock. Flaherty went back to the jail to talk to the suspect again.

"What was the last thing I said to you?"

"That homicide was a science," Davenport answered, his voice that of a naughty little boy talking to his father. In fact, he was a grown man with two toddlers of his own, with no criminal record other than a few drug arrests when he'd gotten embroiled with a wannabe gang in the Pit. His father was the chief probation officer in Cambridge District Court. Davenport was a man who had no business getting mixed up with the teenaged antics of gang bangers who spent all day long skateboarding. But he did it anyway.

"Okay, I was the guy who stabbed her," Davenport blurted.

With that, he confessed to the entire murder. He gave up the names of the two girls who'd held Nachtwey's arms down as Davenport mutilated her with a ten-inch blade. He told Flaherty about Luis Vasquez raping her under a bridge overpass before they'd killed her. He talked about how that same man had nun-chucked the dying girl in the head after getting off during the rape. He even told Flaherty that when Davenport was done stabbing the petite woman, he ran his blood-stained hands through his hair and muttered aloud, "What a rush."

Then the two girls—whose identities were protected after they cooperated with investigators—Davenport, Luis Vasquez, his brother, Ismael, and a junkie named Harold Parker rolled Nachtwey into the Charles River. She was still gasping for breath when her body went over the railway bridge.

Her killers would later describe hearing her head thud off a metal beam before it vanished under the murky waters.

The motive was almost more tragic than the crime. The six were trying to jump-start their own version of the Crips gang, and had decided to kill Nachtwey because her boyfriend had disrespected Davenport in the Pit, in front of other people. In fact, Davenport had only met his victim three hours before he would kneel down and plunge a long knife into her body over and over and over again.

During the Nachtwey murder trial, Assistant District Attorney Patrick Haggan described the six people who killed her: "You will get a glimpse into the type of people who can murder a woman and then go to McDonald's afterward for a hamburger. They killed this victim for no other reason than wanting to start some gang."

But Weinstein scoffed at the prosecutor's description of his client's crew, saying that their association was nothing more than "a small-time, pathetic, hopelessly ridiculous gang." Besides, the suspects were a bit old for gang initiations. Davenport and Parker were both 31 at the time of their trials. Ismael Vasquez was 27, and his brother, Luis, was 23.

"Ismael Vasquez was part of that group, but he is not a murderer," Weinstein said during the trial.

The jury didn't see it that way. The four men involved in the young woman's slaughter were sentenced to life without the possibility of parole. The young women who held down the victim pleaded guilty to manslaughter and will probably spend about 12 to 15 years behind bars.

When sentencing the thugs, Suffolk County Judge Patrick F. Brady told them their crime was "beyond the comprehension of most people."

It was people like that, accused of crimes "beyond the comprehension of most people," that made up a large part of Elliot Weinstein's world long before he met Neil Entwistle.

In fact, Weinstein had questioned Flaherty during cross-examinations in the Nachtwey trial and found him to be a professional law enforcement official. Never did either man imagine that their paths would meet again after Flaherty retired.

It's not a stretch to think that the words "despicable scumbag" may have crossed Flaherty's mind when he thought about Weinstein's newest client on the long roster of maggots the attorney had represented. But clearly, what Joe Flaherty thought of him was not something that would get under Elliot Weinstein's skin or trouble his soul.

Some people in Boston thought he didn't have a soul to begin with.

But that assumption was not entirely right either. In fact, Weinstein was a compassionate man, which is one of the reasons he worked so diligently on behalf of the sick and violent. He knew all too well that life can be upset at such a rapid-fire pace, with an impulsive squeeze of a trigger, an uncontrollable flash of fury, even a misjudged jump. Any misstep can alter the course of someone's entire existence.

His own son, Zach Weinstein, was confined to a wheelchair from diving into shallow waters during a canoe trip after completing his freshman year at Skidmore College, and suffering a debilitating spinal cord injury that left him without any control over his own body whatsoever. Now Zach is living in Needham, Massachusetts, with his mother and father taking care of him. Many defense attorneys say that the younger Weinstein's injury softened his father—but not to the point where he would back down in a courtroom.

Elliot Weinstein made that very clear when he began what many saw as the astonishingly ballsy move of trying to convince a judge to release Neil Entwistle on bail and allow him to await trial at his parents' house in England. That fight was launched only after Weinstein had already convinced a judge that American taxpayers should not only pick up the bills for Entwistle's defense, but also pay $5,000 extra so that his attorney could hire a private investigator. Weinstein argued in his brief that the cash was necessary "for the proper and effective preparation of his defense." But in that argument, Weinstein made an understandable mistake: he confused the killers on his client list and filed the wrong name with the Middlesex County Clerk's Office.

In the affidavit, Weinstein wrote that he represented Omar Denton, who had been accused of shooting a man dead in the South End in 2004. But everyone in the Middlesex Court knew he meant Neil Entwistle. Omar Denton was accused of a bad crime—the daylight murder of a young man who had stepped in when Denton began to administer a very public beating to his girlfriend, and received a bullet in the head for his trouble—but he was not charged with executing a woman and a baby girl.

CHAPTER 16

IT WOULD PROBABLY BE viewed by most defense attorneys as a wise decision not to request bail for your client on the very same day that he is dragged into a courthouse wearing a bulletproof vest and full-body shackles as spectators screech "Burn in hell!" Elliot Weinstein probably assumed that no court would allow Neil Entwistle to walk out on bond.

But by December 5, 2006—nearly a year after Entwistle was arrested—there were other notorious crimes that the public had become obsessed with. It was the holiday season. People were distracted with shopping and parties and family gatherings—things Neil himself had been distracted by just a year earlier.

But with all the bustling that comes with December, Weinstein was hoping that his bid to put up Neil Entwistle's parents' humble home as collateral and allow him to fly home to the United Kingdom to await trial would be quietly considered by a judge without annoying flare-ups in the media and ramblings on talk radio.

Mr. Entwistle submits, as further set below, that there are a combination of strict and specific conditions of pre-trial release that will both assure his appearance as required at trial and will not endanger the safety of any other person in the community.

Mr. Entwistle was arraigned on the above indictment charging him with, inter alia, *two counts of first degree murder. At arraignment, Mr. Entwistle assented to the Court setting no bail, but reserved his right to present his request for bail at a later point.*

And, Weinstein obviously thought, that time was now.

The motion went on to state:

The investigation and indictment of Mr. Entwistle, together with all related court proceedings, have generated unprecedented national and international media coverage. It is anticipated that this motion will itself rekindle media coverage of the allegations against Mr. Entwistle, and about Mr. Entwistle himself. Defense counsel cannot be cowed from our responsibility to zealously represent Mr. Entwistle by fear that a well considered and reasonable proffer of release conditions will be met by a media reaction and cynicism which further erodes Mr. Entwistle's rights to the presumption of innocence and the fundamental right to a fair trial.

So, as the argument went, it was the media's fault that the public hated Neil Entwistle and believed he was guilty—not Weinstein's client's outlandish behavior in the days after the murders, not his flight from the country or his conflicting statements to investigators. Poor Neil Entwistle was the victim of out-of-control tabloid enterprises. Weinstein might well have written that it was all Rupert Murdoch's fault Entwistle was behind bars at all.

While legal authority exists to permit Mr. Entwistle to be held without bail until trial, legal authority also exists which permits and directs this Court to release him subject to conditions.

It is anticipated that the immediate reaction from the Commonwealth to this request for release will be to exclaim that Mr. Entwistle is a danger to the community and a risk of flight evidenced by the circumstances of the shooting death of Rachel and Lillian Entwistle and the fact that Neil Entwistle traveled to his home in the United Kingdom where he was eventually arrested and extradited to Massachusetts. It is exactly these facts which underscore the legitimacy and viability of pre-trial release.

It is undisputed that on January 21, 2006, Neil Entwistle flew from Logan Airport, Boston, to Heathrow Airport, London. It is also undisputed that at the time he traveled there was no legal process preventing travel to his parent's home. Once in the United Kingdom, Mr. Entwistle maintained almost daily telephone contact with Massachusetts State Police investigators. When law enforcement officials decided to have Mr. Entwistle arrested in the United Kingdom and extradited to the United States, Mr. Entwistle facilitated this procedure by waiving his right to challenge the extradition request.

Mr. Entwistle is a man with an unblemished personal history and background. He graduated from public secondary school and scored so well on the highly competitive entrance examination that he was accepted to University of York and graduated in 2002 with a Master in Engineering degree. He has no history or record of prior court involvement in either the United Kingdom or the United States, thus, no history or record of failing to appear for court proceedings.

Besides, Weinstein went on to argue, where could his client possibly be anonymous?

Since on or about January 22, 2006, Neil Entwistle's name, picture, background, and more have been part of a public conversation amongst the populace, and electronic and print media on at least two continents.

This is a man who cannot run and who cannot hide.

Accordingly, Mr. Entwistle requests that this court set the following conditions for his release:

Home Confinement:

Mr. Entwistle be restricted to confinement at his parents' (Clifford Entwistle and Yvonne Entwistle) home at 27 Coleridge Road, Worksop, Nottingham, England.

Custodian:

Clifford Entwistle and Yvonne Entwistle be designated custodians for the purpose of supervision of Neil Entwistle and to report any violation of release conditions to this court and to law enforcement as further set forth below or otherwise ordered by this court.

Electronic GPS Monitor:

Mr. Entwistle will at all times wear an electronic global positioning system (GPS) device to approved by the Commonwealth.

Reporting:

Neil Entwistle be required to report daily by telephone to any combination of: law enforcement officials in Worksop, or elsewhere in the United Kingdom; law enforcement officials in Massachusetts, or elsewhere in the United States; probation officers of this court; officials of the Department of State and United States Embassy and/or other representative of the United States government; and, to report in person to any local government authority be it court or law enforcement in Worksop or elsewhere as deemed appropriate.

Oh, and the parents would also give the title to their home to the court, Weinstein added in an addendum.

Waiver of Extradition:

Neil Entwistle will execute any and all waivers of extradition from the United Kingdom to the United States to the satisfaction of the Middlesex County District Attorney's Office.

No Contact:

Refrain from any contact with any prospective witness in this case and said persons to be identified in writing by the Middlesex County District Attorney's Office.

Security for Appearance:

An appearance for bond with terms satisfactory to the Commonwealth to be executed by Neil Entwistle, Clifford Entwistle, and Yvonne Entwistle. A mortgage in favor of the Clerk, Middlesex County Superior Court, or other designee of the Commonwealth, to the property at 27 Coleridge Road, Worksop, Nottingham, England;

A deed which, in case of default, conveys title to said Clerk, or other designee of the Commonwealth, together with an agreement that said deed be held in escrow until otherwise ordered by this court.

The proposed conditions of release are designed to provide reasonable and adequate assurance that Mr. Entwistle will appear for court proceedings as required and will not endanger the safety of any person or the community. Accordingly, Mr. Entwistle requests that, after hearing on the motion, the court set these or any further conditions it deems necessary as conditions as pre-trial release.

As the Middlesex County Clerk stamped the date on the request and put it in the file, he shrugged his shoulders and declared to a visitor in the office, "We call these the 'Yeah, right' motions." And that's exactly what Middlesex County prosecutors argued in a brief bail hearing. They didn't need to present too strong a case why Neil Entwistle should not be leaving the country any time soon, so prosecutors merely used the *We don't think so* fight. *Nice try, Weinstein*, Assistant District Attorney Michael Fabbri, who was now trying the case for Middlesex County, likely thought, as he watched the infamous defense attorney trying his best to posture for yet another accused killer.

"I don't think I exaggerate when I say to you that Neil Entwistle is not a man who can run and hide. The conditions we propose are strict, very strict," and besides, if he did flee, his parents would be homeless, Weinstein argued before the judge.

"It's not an off-the-wall request," Weinstein said, as his client stood strangely still and silent beside him, dressed in an ill-fitting charcoal-colored suit with a pink shirt and tie. "It's a minor request. It's not a burden."

In court, Fabbri simply said that Neil Entwistle had shown a "clear pattern of flight and unreliability.

"He fled the scene immediately . . . without seeking any medical help after purportedly finding his wife and his daughter," Fabbri said. "He had no ties to the United States."

Besides, Fabbri said, why would the taxpayers want to incur any other expenses associated with Neil

Entwistle's defense—like making sure he didn't flee before trial?

Joe Flaherty, who was still acting as the spokesman for Priscilla and Joe Matterazzo, made it clear to the court—as well as the media, who immediately discovered Weinstein's attempts to bring his client home for the holidays, and, as the lawyer had feared, promptly reported it and vilified the effort—that Rachel and Lilly's loved ones were "vehemently opposed" to any freedom for the man accused of killing them.

"He should stay right where he is until the trial," Flaherty said. "I can't even fathom that the judge will entertain it. He's not even a U.S. citizen, and there is the strength of the case and the investigation itself."

The clerk's projection was the right one. Weeks later, just days before Christmas, Superior Court Justice Peter Lauriat denied Weinstein's bid, writing in his order:

> *After a hearing, and upon consideration of the memorandum from the defendant and the arguments of counsel for both parties, the Defendant's Motion to Set Conditions of Pretrial release is DENIED.*
>
> *The provisions of the Bail Reform Act do not extend to person charged with murder in the first degree.*

Lauriat then ticked off a couple of case law examples to prove his point:

Since the statute does not apply, the question of bail for a person charged with murder in the first degree is a matter of discretion.

Upon consideration of all the facts and circumstances of this case, as presented by counsel for the Commonwealth and the defendant at the hearing on this motion, the court concludes, in the sound exercise of its discretion and consistent with the interests of justice, that the defendant's release on conditions of bail which would allow him to reside in England pending trial in this case is neither warranted nor appropriate.

Deep down, even Elliot Weinstein expected this ruling. He had hinted at it in his own motion. Yes, indeed, the Commonwealth "exclaimed" the very words uttered by the courthouse clerk: *Yeah, right.* Weinstein did put on a brave face for reporters, telling them, "We're disappointed with the judge's decision. We appreciate the hearing and the full and fair consideration that he gave our request."

Besides, in all likelihood, Neil Entwistle was home for the holidays. It was all too likely that prison would be his home for a very, very long time to come.

CHAPTER 17

THIS KID SURE HAS a lot of balls, Middlesex County Sheriff James DiPaola thought when he heard about the letter that guards found in Neil Entwistle's cell at the medical unit of the Middlesex jail the day after the judge denied his attempt to await trial in the relative safety of his parents' home.

"This may be my last letter," Neil wrote to Yvonne and Cliff Entwistle. "I have nothing to look forward to."

His next request was so outlandish, Priscilla Matterazzo actually considered getting a court order to make sure that nothing like this could happen, ever:

> *If I die, I want to be cremated and have my ashes sprinkled over Rachel and Lilly's grave.*

DiPaola could not have a suicide in his prison. No way. A dead prisoner equals a lot of aggravation, no matter who it is. Committees are formed by human rights activists. Investigations are launched. Jail administrators are blamed.

"He never actually threatens to kill himself," Di-Paola said. "But there's tell-tale signs of depression.

"There were some key words that caught the attention of the officers," he said. "It included burial instructions. It wasn't, per se, I'm going to hang myself; I'm going to harm myself. It was more of a conversation about him being depressed."

Still, the sheriff was not taking any chances. He decided right then and there that he would ship Neil Entwistle out for a psychiatric evaluation at Bridgewater State Hospital, nicknamed "Bridgey" by virtually everyone in Massachusetts. Bridgewater was also the place where the Department of Correction housed sexual predators, rapists, pedophiles and other deviants so dangerous that Massachusetts lawmakers had successfully passed a bill that would allow the state's parole board to "civilly commit" violent sex offenders beyond their sentences if they were deemed likely to repeat their crimes.

The news could have come as some relief for Entwistle. After all, he had been locked up in the medical unit's cell for more than ten months without a single visitor besides his defense attorneys, and very few distractions. His hints at suicide would at least earn him a change of scenery, even if it was just from seeing psychopaths and prison guards at Middlesex Jail to seeing drooling psychopaths and prison guards in hospital scrubs at Bridgewater State. The letter may have been the cagiest idea Entwistle had come up with yet. After all, he should have been well aware that his mail was monitored, and he was smart enough to know that the

sheriff and the command staff at the prison did not
want any dead bodies in their cells. It was unlikely,
however, that Entwistle realized his suicide scare
would prompt a mandatory search of all the cells in
the medical unit—including his.

And that search would put him in very intimate
contact with another prisoner who just happened to
loathe baby killers. In fact, that 33-year-old prisoner,
Eben Sewall Howard, a sinewy man with brown hair
who stood five-foot-ten and weighed 170 pounds, and
had the cold, dead eyes of the heavily medicated, just
happened to hate anyone accused of hurting a child.
Howard was in prison for allegedly fatally strangling
the new boyfriend of his son's mother down in Jack-
sonville, North Carolina, and just like Entwistle he
would be waiting for his trial well into 2009.

A guard named Robert McCarthy would later describe Howard's meeting with Entwistle in a Middlesex County sheriff's report:

> *During cell search of the medical unit at ap-
> proximately 9:10 p.m., I was watching inmate
> Entwistle while Sgt. Sullivan and CO [Correc-
> tion Officer] Lee searched the cells. Howard
> was let out and I observed him also.*
>
> *Howard calmly threw a kick at Entwistle's ab-
> domen. I then restrained Howard and was able
> to back him into the corner and instructed En-
> twistle to back off into medical. Entwistle com-
> plied while Howard resisted vigorously. Either
> Deputy Costello or Sullivan's right arm reached*

*over my right shoulder and restrained Howard's
head. I was then able to let go of Howard's
torso and apply a wrist lock on Howard's right
wrist and take him to the floor with the assistance of Sullivan and Lee. Howard was cuffed
and seen by medical and brought to the 137 cell
by CO McBride and me. Entwistle was seen by
medical.*

The kick was ferocious enough that Entwistle took
a step back away from his assailant and fell to the
ground. A nurse in the medical unit helped him to his
feet and examined him, but found no major injuries.

It was not Howard's first offense behind bars, his
attorney, Jeffrey Denner, acknowledged, adding the
caveat that his client committed all of his alleged
crimes while mentally ill. In 2004, he'd been charged
with assaulting a prison guard in a Brockton, Massachusetts, lockup—that came after he was charged
with attacking an elderly black janitor who was mop-
ping the floor in the psychiatric ward of a hospital.
Before Howard's mind began to deteriorate with
schizophrenia, he'd held a job as a sales representative at the *Boston Herald*, the second-largest daily
newspaper in Massachusetts.

Denner said the attack was the work of a "very
troubled young man who has severe mental problems.
He's not a man who is dealing with rational thought."

Privately, Denner thought that his client had kicked
Neil Entwistle because the Englishman was being
held for a crime that was unthinkable, even to a para-

noid schizophrenic who was on high doses of anti-psychotic drugs. Howard's father, Rick, a prominent attorney, said that it was more likely the schizophrenia that prompted his son's attack than any resentment that Entwistle was charged with killing a baby.

No matter what the cause, the boot left Entwistle with a softball-size bruise on his soft, white stomach. If he wasn't really suicidal when he'd penned that letter to his parents, the kick might have pushed him to that edge for real.

The following morning, December 21, 2006, Neil Entwistle was lethargic as guards pulled a bullet-proof vest over his head—again. They slipped his sweaty hands into cuffs and attached those to a full-body shackle around his waist. His ankles were put back in the manacles, which dragged a chain between his legs as he walked. Prison guards placed a hand on the top of his head as they pushed him down and into a Department of Correction van for the forty-four-mile trip to Bridgewater State Hospital. The state's correction department had a special wing in the hospital.

Neil Entwistle was not the only accused killer who had made the trip that week. Of the 381 prisoners at Middlesex County jail, twenty-one of them were receiving treatment for depression at Bridgewater during Christmas week. It was not uncommon around the holidays for even the most violent cons to reevaluate their lives and become overwhelmed by a sense of extreme loneliness.

Entwistle was held at the hospital for three weeks,

at which point Department of Correction officials felt that he was ready to return to general population at the Middlesex jail. He did not show any signs of a truly suicidal man, and the brief break he had sleeping on a softer bed with seemingly less dangerous inmates around him had to come to an end. "He does not appear to be a threat to himself or to others," DiPaola explained to the press.

On January 10, 2007, three prison guards put him back in his body armor and shackles and escorted him back to his tiny cell in the medical unit and continued his solitary existence of reading the Bible, praying and staring into space. Only now he was not alone. DiPaola said that in addition to the jail's cameras, there would be an around-the-clock guard posted by the cell to eyeball Entwistle. "There will always be a human being outside," the sheriff explained.

After all, Howard was still in the same unit. And while they were separated by tons of concrete and never out of their cells at the same time, the sheriff certainly did not want another assault on the most high-profile prisoner in his system. When Howard was brought to court, where he pleaded not guilty to assaulting Neil Entwistle, his victim was back in the medical unit waiting for time to pass.

During all this excitement in the Middlesex jail, Elliot Weinstein had suddenly become camera shy. The same attorney who, at Entwistle's first court appearance, had posed for a picture with his legs crossed, showing off the cowboy boots tucked under the leg of his tailored suit pants, had become uncharacteristically unavailable for comment.

In the coming weeks it would be made clear why Weinstein had developed his drastic change of heart regarding the maintenance of his own high profile.

CHAPTER 18

JUST DAYS AFTER NEIL Entwistle was returned to his cell in the Middlesex jail's medical unit, the prosecutor who had been at the forefront of the case against him would make Massachusetts history.

Martha Coakley—wearing her trademark high-heel pumps—was sworn in as the state's first female attorney general in a well-attended ceremony in her rural hometown of North Adams, in the Berkshire Mountains of western Massachusetts. Being the first woman to hold the highest law enforcement office position was not Coakley's focus, however, and she was determined to make sure people knew that.

"It's not a big deal," Coakley said over and over again. "I wanted to do the job, not win the election."

And winning the election was no big deal for Coakley. She'd run unopposed in the Democratic primary and then walloped her Republican opponent. An attractive woman whose hair was a bottle straw-berry blonde and who cut a striking figure in her power suits, Coakley was humbled as she stood at a podium in North Adams and vowed that she would take on the corrupt contractors of the multi-billion-dollar Big Dig project. The Big Dig was a real challenge, a legendary Boston boondoggle that could cement Coakley's place in Massachusetts history for a prosecution that was far more important than putting a killer in jail. Contractors on the job were accused of bilking taxpayers out of millions of dollars, cutting corners to such an outrageous degree that their shoddy workmanship had led to the death of a Boston woman, crushed to death when concrete panel fell from the ceiling in one of the tunnels.

Prosecuting Neil Entwistle would be left in the hands of one of her former colleagues at the Office of the Middlesex District Attorney, Gerald Leone.

Leone was a true hardscrabble prosecutor. He'd been born and raised in the gritty Boston neighborhood of Brighton under the watchful eye of his father, a high school football coach, and his mother, who was a homemaker. He'd worked his way through Harvard University and Suffolk Law School, paying his bills by working as a counselor at the Pine Street Inn, a sprawling Boston homeless shelter.

His career in the Middlesex District Attorney's office came after a long stint in the Massachusetts Attorney General's office where he was the chief of the criminal bureau, leading more than eighty attorneys, state police detectives and narcotic cops. Leone also worked for the federal government as the first assistant United States Attorney, managing investigations into terrorism in the terrible months after the 9-11 attacks. Before long, Leone became the Department of

Justice's first ever Anti-Terrorism Task Force Coordinator for Massachusetts.

He earned a name for himself in 2003 when he successfully prosecuted "shoe bomber" Richard Reid, who had attempted to detonate explosives in his sneaker aboard American Airlines Flight 63 on December 22, 2001. After a stewardess smelled smoke hovering around Reid's seat, she approached the long-haired, bearded Brit.

"What are you doing, sir?" asked the flight attendant, Hermis Moutardier.

Reid responded by lunging at her. In his lap, there was a single shoe with a fuse leading into the sole. He was holding a lit match. Moutardier tried wrestling the bomb away from Reid, but he pushed her to the floor. He bit another flight attendant's thumb.

The screams of the stewardesses got the attention of passengers, all of whom were still rattled by the murder of thousands of people just months earlier on September 11. The men around Reid's seat leapt into action. They tackled the six-foot-four Reid, and bound him with a pair of plastic handcuffs, wrapped his arms with a seatbelt extension and even used headphone cords as extra protection on his hands. A doctor aboard the flight used a syringe to pump him full of Valium that was found in the flight kit on the plane.

Two fighter jets then escorted the plane into Boston's Logan International Airport. Once it landed, the Department of Justice handed the case to the Massachusetts United States Attorney's Office. It was then that Gerry Leone was able to prove his prosecutorial mettle after he became the lead federal prosecutor in what would be dubbed the *United States of America* vs. *Richard Colvin Reid*, a case that after years of investigation was presented in Boston's federal court in 2003. Reid had been born in Britain, the son of an English mother and a Jamaican father. He'd converted to Islam in an English prison where he was serving time for petty violent crimes connected to his youth as a street thug.

One of the first coups Leone won in the case was to deny Reid access to news media, after his attorneys filed a motion that would allow him to have both a radio and a copy of *Time* magazine in his federal prison cell. Leone argued that "allowing Reid to access and obtain incoming, unmonitored, unaltered communications without delay may provoke or motivate Reid to act or send codable messages outside the facility." Reid's real motivation for wanting access to the media was clearly the attention that he was receiving during his trial. as he would often stand up and engage the court in long, rambling tirades where he would declare himself a martyr who would surely be rewarded with a bevy of virgins in the afterlife.

Leone wrote in his response:

Reid, as demonstrated by his conduct and words, awaits the Jan. 30, 2003 sentencing as a committed and dedicated international terrorist who engaged in a martyrdom mission within three months of September 11th as part of a terrorist campaign against this nation—a campaign which deploys techniques of stealth and

secrecy, including codes and hidden messages;
and as an admitted member of Al Qaeda, who
had pledged to serve Osama Bin Laden, is an
enemy of his country, who used the explosive
device in this case as an act of war intending to
blow up the plane and all the 180 people on the
plane—including himself.

The judge ruled in his favor and Reid went without his radio and *Time* subscription. Already, Reid had been banned from having most commissary items available to other prisoners, including combs, condiments, spices, batteries, pens and pencils and some types of hygienic products because of his adept bomb-making skills. He was being held at Massachusetts Correctional Institution at Cedar Junction, in the Disciplinary Disorders Unit, under the eye of the state's hardest correction officers.

Leone won the case in January of 2003 when Reid decided to plead guilty to all eight counts logged against him, including attempted use of a weapon of mass destruction, attempted homicide, and placing an explosive device on an aircraft. By then, Leone had proven that

Reid was not unassisted in his efforts to destroy
Flight 63; and ... his choice of an American
target was a deliberate and calculated act of in-
ternational terrorism.

Reid had assistance in building and obtain-
ing the explosive device, and preparing for and
executing his mission in this case; Reid's travels

and activity in advance of his attempted bomb-
ing are detailed in his preparatory trip report
that was located on a computer that was found
in Afghanistan; and Reid's post arrest state-
ments to federal agents detailed his anti-
American beliefs.

An unrepentant Reid received three sentences of
life in prison, in addition to one 30-year and four 20-
year terms, to be served consecutively—as well as $2
million in fines, plus restitution and special assess-
ments. He is currently confined to ADX Florence, a
"supermax," or super-maximum security prison in
Colorado.

The Richard Reid trial would catapult the career of
a dogged prosecutor into the top job at the Office of
the Middlesex District Attorney. And there, for the
third time in his illustrious career, Gerald Leone
would be trying a British-born national for crimes
against Americans. First Louise Woodward, then
Richard Reid, and now Neil Entwistle.

Gerry Leone certainly had no doubts that the Middlesex County District Attorney had charged the right
man with the crime. He said as much on countless national television shows.

When he was interviewed about the murders,
Leone was a private citizen free to expound on his
theories about the rock-solid case prosecutors had
against the suspect. Even if he was running for the
Middlesex County District Attorney's slot, which
would make him responsible for trying Neil Entwistle, Leone could pontificate as long as he didn't

point fingers. After all, Leone's familiarity with the case went beyond his role in law enforcement. He lived in the town of Hopkinton with his wife, Wendy, and their two children—a boy and a girl, just as the census for the town predicted for most of the families that settled in the suburb. The fact that he lived where the crime had occurred, coupled with his criminal expertise, made Leone the perfect pundit for the national media's obsession with the case.

"The presumptive side of this case is focused on Neil Entwistle, that he had something to do with this, if not was responsible for the murders," Leone commented on MSNBC on February 2, 2006, days before Neil was even tracked and arrested.

Three nights later, Leone had this to say on Fox News: "Any time you have a homicide, especially deaths of this nature, it's unsettling. It's unsettling in a town like Hopkinton, where they're not used to this kind of violent crime. And the domestic violence component that is part of the presumptive side of this case is unsettling for anyone."

After the arrest, Leone ripped apart the statements Entwistle had made to investigators in the *Boston Herald*. "Any time someone who is charged makes a statement, they narrow the possibilities for themselves."

A day earlier on CNN—after Entwistle had agreed to be extradited from England—Leone made these comments: "It's what I call a theory of half-truths, half-lies. I mean, as he learns about some of the facts and some of the evidence, those are the truths. But as he starts to fill in the holes with his version of the story, those are the half-lies. So, you get half-truths, which are the things that we know to be true, but the half-lies are, when he talks, it's belied by the facts and by the evidence."

While what Gerry Leone was saying was true, those televised comments would come back to haunt him. A year later, Elliot Weinstein filed a brief that essentially said there was no way in hell that his client would be able to receive a fair trial and hinted that he was considering asking a judge to boot Leone from the case. After all, Weinstein argued, the lead prosecutor had shot off his mouth about Neil Entwistle on national TV. "I respect Gerry Leone," Weinstein said, "notwithstanding that media comments that were made that have impacted Mr. Entwistle's right to a fair trial are something that we must evaluate in our obligation to properly and zealously represent Mr. Entwistle."

State Trooper Joe Flaherty, who was still acting as the spokesman for Rachel's mother and step-father, quickly defended Leone: "He has been careful in what he said. He wasn't saying anyone was guilty or innocent."

It hardly mattered what Leone had said about Neil Entwistle and whether it crossed the line. There was one singular truth in what Weinstein was saying about his client: It was going to be very hard to find a potential juror in Massachusetts who thought that the unemployed, sex-crazed Brit was not the gunman who'd murdered his wife and child.

CHAPTER 19

AFTER GERRY LEONE TOOK office in Middlesex County, he never spoke publicly about the Neil Entwistle case again. In fact, he avoided reporters entirely—fearful, perhaps, that Elliot Weinstein's argument would be successful, if not to a judge, at least to potential jurors.

Middlesex County is a fairly liberal place. For most people in Massachusetts, Cambridge is considered a bastion of liberal thinking, a city filled with residents who lean so far to the left, many complain that they might as well be Communists. In fact, the city is commonly referred to as the People's Republic of Cambridge. And the surrounding towns that make up Middlesex County are filled with enough liberals that Weinstein's whining that Entwistle could not get a fair trial because of the publicity in the case might work on them. The last thing Leone wanted in his new position was an acquittal on what seemed to be a slam-dunk case. They had the perpetrator's DNA, they had his story that investigators had already punched full of holes, and they had the court of public opinion, which had already convicted the guy. Besides, Leone was a politician to the core, right down to his appearance, with his perfectly coiffed hair and permanently implanted smile. He could not afford to lose this one and become a laughing stock to voters, who might eventually elevate him to higher office.

Leone had plenty to keep him busy while Entwistle cooled his heels in jail awaiting trial. In March of 2006, there was a mysterious double-homicide in the sleepy, blue-collar town of Wakefield—the same town where Michael "Mucko" McDermott had gone on a rampage in 2000. The owner of a concrete plant came into work and found his 39-year-old son and namesake, Michael Zammitti Jr., slumped to the floor, shot dead with a single blast to the head. Then he found the body of a worker, Chester Roberts, 51, who had been shot in the back fleeing the gunman. Months later, investigators found the alleged killer, Sean Fitzpatrick, in the rural lake resort town of Freedom, New Hampshire. Fitzpatrick had been "pursuing a relationship with Zammitti's wife," but in the weeks before the homicides, Michelle Zammitti told her one-time lover that she was interested in saving her marriage. The couple had three children and lived in an opulent house on the upscale side of Wakefield during the winter, and summered in a New Hampshire cottage. It would be too complicated to give all that up, she told Fitzpatrick, who then apparently snapped and killed Zammitti. Poor Chester Roberts was a hapless victim who'd wandered into an execution at exactly the wrong time.

Leone's office was building a strong case against

Sean Fitzpatrick, and was hoping that Michelle Zammitti would be a witness against him. Turning a cheating wife into a witness for the prosecution was never easy, and Leone himself had a hand in the trial prep. Fitzpatrick, to this day, steadfastly maintains his innocence.

Another case that was taking up a lot of prosecutors' time was being brought against a Brazilian couple who had turned their basement apartment in Framingham into an illegal liposuction parlor. Apparently, none of their neighbors noticed the constant flow of women who would come in and out of the "office" of Luiz Carlos Ribeiro and his wife, Ana Maria Miranda Ribeiro—until police stormed the place after a 24-year-old woman died from one of their procedures. Neither of the Ribeiros had a medical license, but they did have a long client list of patients who paid up to $7,000 to have fat sucked from their legs or bellies. It was going to be an easy case to prove, but it was still time-consuming for Leone's office. Eventually, Ana Maria pleaded guilty and agreed to testify against her husband at his trial. The couple has since divorced.

Then there was the Somerville cop arrested for raping a 2-year-old girl with a curling iron. The child was injured severely enough that she was admitted to the hospital for days, and her mother called the police. It was later discovered that the 31-year-old officer, Keith Winfield, allegedly "assaulted the child with a hot object, resulting in serious injury," while babysitting. When details of what Winfield allegedly did to the girl hit the papers, Leone's office had to make sure that none of the law enforcement officers who would be handling him during transports to court or behind bars helped him somehow harm himself. But the case was a political hot potato for reasons that went beyond the horrifying nature of the crime, or the reaction of his fellow cops. He resigned from the force and was sentenced to life in prison after being found guilty.

It had taken Leone's predecessor, Martha Coakley, ten months to arrest and indict the Somerville cop, a delay that prompted many critics to start griping that Winfield was receiving preferential treatment. Winfield's father was a business agent for the New England Regional Council of Carpenters, who had financially supported Coakley's campaign for attorney general. She denied any wrongdoing and tried to blame the grand jury for the delay: "After an extensive investigation, the case was presented to the grand jury, resulting in the indictment against Officer Winfield." But many people weren't buying that any investigation should take that long when the girl was only with one person—Winfield—and the swirling allegations about favoritism and impropriety in the case tainted Coakley's win when she was sworn in as attorney general. Nonetheless, Leone was not going to let politics get in the way of prosecution, and he was carrying on with the case.

And, then there were the wins that his office was celebrating. There was the conviction of Michael Bizanowicz, a sex offender who'd broken into the home of his neighbor, and raped 34-year-old Joanne Presti as her young daughter screamed. Then he slashed their throats. The case was a watershed for

Leone, as many people in Massachusetts were out-raged that a predator like Bizanowicz, who had al-ready been convicted of raping a child, was able to be free to walk the streets at all. The murders prompted lawmakers to draft the Joanne and Alyssa Act—a bill that would tighten legislation about the monitoring of sex offenders. Their killer had been classified Level Three, the most dangerous, but had still managed to live in relative anonymity in the suburban town of Woburn, where he had been able to target Presti and her daughter with an eerie ease. Leone also put away a firebug from Cambridge who'd set fire to a building that sparked a fatal blaze, killing an elderly woman and her 8-year-old granddaughter. He also won an-other conviction for Vuthy Seng, a Lowell, Massachu-setts, thug who had convinced a court that he was owed a retrial for the 1995 conviction on charges that he had killed three young boys. Seng may have con-vinced a court to grant him a new trial, but yet another Middlesex County jury put him away.

In a speech in front of a New England Bar Associa-tion group that April, which Leone's flack promoted as "Leone Highlights First One Hundred Days," the new district attorney crowed about his successes and ac-complishments during his first four months in office.

"When I took office, I promised to build on the proud legacy and tradition of excellence in the Mid-dlesex District Attorney's office by implementing a dual approach: coordinating to intervene and prevent crime on the front end while protecting our most vul-nerable by fairly and effectively prosecuting cases," Leone told the assembled lawyers during his speech.

"While we certainly have been challenged early on, our office has risen to meet those challenges.

"In stressing to each of our attorneys that we are not only professional prosecutors, but are also progressive public servants . . ." Leone said, they will become ingrained in that community—handling cases, working on community-based intervention and prevention initiatives . . .

"As you can see, it has been a busy and successful, first one hundred days. But there is much work to be done. . . . I can assure you that our dedicated team understands that we have been entrusted with an opportunity to serve . . . We are committed to passionately fighting for the victims of crime while maintaining that sacred public trust and confidence."

For the lawyers, Leone's words had the blah-blah-blah tone of a campaign speech. It had all been said before by each and every politician who ran for any of the eleven elected district attorney positions in Massachusetts. Like the media who quietly attended the luncheon, the lawyers were hoping to hear some inside scoop on the Entwistle case and how Gerry Leone planned to prosecute it.

But Leone did not say a single word about Neil Entwistle. It was almost as if he knew that Elliot Weinstein had another card up his sleeve, and Leone was not going to jinx himself by bringing up the name of the most notorious accused killer currently slated to be tried in Middlesex County.

It was a good call, because within weeks of that speech, Weinstein filed another staggeringly brazen brief. This time he wanted the court to throw out all the evidence investigators had garnered from the Entwistles' home during the search for the missing family, because Neil had not given them permission to enter his house.

CHAPTER 20

THE LAST TIME COURT spectators saw Neil Entwistle inside a courtroom the year before, he had certainly looked dazed. But on this spring day, April 23, 2007, even Rachel and Lillian's loved ones sitting in the first row of the courtroom sucked in a surprised breath when Neil shuffled into the courtroom wearing an ill-fitting, wrinkled suit. Probably something that Elliot Weinstein had purchased for another accused killer's court appearance, and kept in the back of his truck for just these kinds of days. Neil certainly didn't have the cash flow to buy his own suit, and there was not a single person in the United States who was likely to buy one for him. Neil's face was spotty with tiny pricks of acne, like a diaper rash had spread across his cheeks. His skin was gluey and puffed. Clearly he had been subjected to a long spate of bad nutrition and apparent high doses of anti-depressants. His hands were cuffed in the front. He didn't dare look at those gathered in the front row, silk roses pinned to their chests as a memorial to Rachel and baby Lilly. Instead, his glazed-over eyes darted around the room nervously, not resting anywhere, but working hard to look as if he were casually evaluating the old wood and the portraits of former judges that hung on the walls.

Behind him, one of Joseph Matterazzo's sons glared at Entwistle's back. He had been one of the men who had tried to teach Entwistle how to shoot when the boys went target practicing. He knew his father was happy with Priscilla, and he had wanted to help welcome his step-sister's new husband into the fold. Like his father, the younger Matterazzo was horrified every time he thought about the fact that he had fired the same .22-caliber handgun that Entwistle was accused of using to kill Rachel and Lilly.

At this point, Joe and Priscilla Matterazzo did not want to see Neil Entwistle in court—in fact, it would have been fine with them if they never had to look at his lying, deceitful face ever again. If anything, they would wait until his trial in the coming months. Besides, Joe Flaherty knew that some of the Hopkinton investigators, who'd found the bodies by following a foul odor, could be forced to testify about that grisly night, and he gently advised the couple to stay home. No need for them to hear the kind of details that Flaherty had worked hard over the past fifteen months to keep from them.

Neil's parents had still not made the trip from London to support him, and told people in Worksop they had not decided whether to travel to Boston for the upcoming trial. They did tell a highly regarded British newspaper, the *Guardian*, that they believed that Neil was wrongly accused and would be acquitted.

"Our Neil is innocent, totally one hundred percent innocent," his mother, Yvonne, blurted to a reporter staked outside her home. "Every second of every minute of every hour of every day, we think of Neil, Rachel and little Lillian. And if it wasn't for family and friends, especially friends who are remarkable people, we would not be able to face each day."

After a court officer gently guided Neil Entwistle to a defense table where he was flanked by Elliot Weinstein and another attorney, he sat down and began to stare at the table. He entered a signed affidavit that became part of the court record that day:

> *I, Neil Entwistle, state the following to be true to the best of my information and belief:*
> 1. *In January, 2006, I resided at 6 Cubs Way [sic], Hopkinton, Massachusetts;*
> 2. *I am told that the police entered my home on two occasions: January 21, 2006 and January 22, 2006;*
> 3. *I did not give any law enforcement officer or any other person permission to enter my residence on or after January 21, 2006;*
> 4. *I did not give my consent for any law enforcement officer or any other person to search through my house or belongings on or after January 21, 2006;*
> 5. *I never knowingly or voluntarily waived any of my constitutional rights regarding the January 21, 2006 and January 22, 2006 searches of my home.*

The document was signed in cursive—a signature that a handwriting analyst could have had a field day with. The girlish script began with just an *N* with a loopy dot for the first name followed by his last name with the *t* crossed from the end.

It had been submitted along with Weinstein's argument that Hopkinton police "broke into" Entwistle's house—twice—to search it without permission. It was an interesting legal challenge, and defense attorneys across Massachusetts—including Jeffrey Denner, who represented Eben Howard, the man accused of kicking Entwistle in the stomach—supported Weinstein's efforts to have the evidence seized at 6 Cubs Path thrown out, saying that without a warrant the cops had no probable cause to search the house.

"Simply because a family is missing doesn't alter the Constitution. To search a house, you have to have probable cause. And if there was cause, that should have been presented to a judge," Denner said. "That's why we go to them, so we're not relying on the unfettered decisions of police."

So the well-being checks conducted by the Hopkinton police when they jimmied open the door with the Blockbuster card and searched it the first night, and the follow-up search the next night upon prompting from Rachel's mother and her best friend, were at best unwelcome intrusions and at worst a blatant disregard for Neil Entwistle's civil rights. "Hopkinton Police had no valid justification for entering the Entwistle home without a warrant, and thus their search was unconstitutional," Weinstein wrote.

In his memorandum, with the Fourth Amendment as

his rationale, Weinstein strongly urged a judge to throw out: "all evidence seized by police on Jan. 23, 25, 27, 31 and Feb. 8, March 14, 23, May 1 or 11th and Aug. 21." In addition, he wanted "all evidence seized from computers, a Palm Pilot and 'jump drives' also tossed from the case. Weinstein's brief went for broke, and asked a judge to disallow any investigative evidence gathered during the first two searches of the Entwistle home, ten subsequent searches, Entwistle's car and everything on his computer files, claiming that it had all been seized illegally. Also, any statements that he made to police, any evidence seized by cops in the United Kingdom, any incriminating documents found on his jump drive or anything found in his vehicle—like the Dasani water bottle that had provided the DNA to investigators that linked Neil Entwistle to the murder weapons.

Of course, the evidence that Weinstein wanted suppressed was the most damaging against Neil Entwistle. For a self-described computer genius, Neil had not thought to clean up what was on his computers' hard drives or on storage discs around the house. A judge had already granted a search warrant based on State Police Trooper Michael Banks' affidavit stating the facts of the case:

> It . . . appears that Neil Entwistle is knowledge-able about computers; he apparently developed his own family website, rachelandneil.org; he sought employment at two companies in Massachusetts, one of which . . . is an electronic design company, and the other . . . which is a developer of broadcast facility remote control

*systems; and Neil Entwistle either began or is
attempting to begin his own hi-tech company,
"ENT Embedded New Technologies," which,
from its website, claims to provide complex
computer services. In addition to the two laptop
computers and palm pilots . . . I also observed a
number of data storage discs at the residence.*

*I have examined the Entwistle family website,
www.rachelandneil.org. This website lists four
email addresses for contacting Neil and Rachel
Entwistle*

But Trooper Banks also found that Neil Entwistle
had two additional email accounts that were apparently secreted from his wife, which led the investigator to write:

*I know that persons who have committed a serious crime such as murder may be in contact
with friends, family members or accomplices
via email, seeking assistance, advice, refuge, or
otherwise providing information that will assist
law enforcement in its investigation of the
crime. In addition, an examination of Neil and
Rachel Entwistle's email accounts may provide
information about the status of their finances,
or may identify other, heretofore unknown persons who may have information that could assist law enforcement in this investigation.*

Banks also wanted to know if Entwistle had been
monitoring his own media coverage, getting a sick

thrill from the idea that he was the subject of sensational headlines and television talk shows across the globe:

> *Furthermore, I know from my years of investigating homicides and other serious crimes that perpetrators often use the Internet to research and, in effect trouble shoot murder plans and their efforts to cover up such plans once carried out. I further know that once the crime has been accomplished, perpetrators often use the computer and the Internet in an ongoing attempt to monitor the investigation through the media and . . . search and review materials in their efforts to continue to cover up and conceal the crime.*

Then Banks ticked off a list of the items that were seized from the Entwistle home during the searches on January 23 and January 25 in 2006—which produced the bulk of the evidence that Weinstein wanted to suppress:

> *a. One San Disc USB Drive, labeled "Neil" . . . ;*
> *b. One San Disc USB Jump Drive, labeled "ENT" . . . ;*
> *c. One San Disc (blue), labeled "Main" . . . ;*
> *d. One Disgo Lite 128 M USB Jump Drive labeled "Backup" . . . ;*
> *e. One San Disc Kingston Technology, labeled "Backup" . . . ;*
> *f. Twelve writable CD ROM disks located inside an Avery Mailing Lists label box;*

g. *Fifty-six writable CD Rom disks inside black Logic CD case;*

h. *One gold colored CD ROM labeled in pen with "X" or "4" . . . ;*

i. *Two 3½' floppy disks with Mass. State Police Evidence # 2006-110-0019:20; and*

j. *Twelve CD ROM disks, Verabitm, with Mass. State Police Evidence # 2006-110-0019:22.*

Also when Joseph Mattarazzo [sic] voluntarily gave me his HP Pavillion computer to search, he also gave me two 3½' floppy disks, one green with no label and one black with label . . .

Banks then revealed that two cops from the town of Medford, Lieutenant John McLean and Detective Lawrence James, who were extremely prolific at locating files that had been deleted but remained on the hard drive, were the investigators who'd located the debauchery that Neil Entwistle was engaging in after his wife fell asleep:

evidence that on January 16, 2006, Neil Entwistle visited "Adult Friend Finder," a website which appears to me to be dedicated to assisting subscribers in finding sexual partners through Internet chat rooms, personal advertisements and other services, and that Entwistle made attempts to contact persons on that site;

. . . evidence that on January 18, 2006, Neil Entwistle conducted an internet search for "escort services," and that he obtained names and

*addresses of various providers of escort serv-
ices in the Boston and Worcester metropolitan
areas, including ones with such names as "Eye
Candy Entertainment," "Exotic Express," and
"Sweet Temptations;" one such listing, "Blonde
Beauties Escort Svc" including a telephone
number and a Yahoo map of their location in
Worcester, but did not include the street address;*

*Evidence that on January 18, 2006, Neil En-
twistle searched Yahoo Maps and/or other internet map services to locate numerous specific
streets and neighborhoods in the Worcester area*

It is now increasingly common for people to search
the Internet for ways to kill people. In fact, as Neil
Entwistle sat awaiting trial, a pretty brunette fertility
clinic nurse from New Jersey, Melanie McGuire, was
being tried for shooting her husband dead exactly ten
days after she entered the words "how to commit
murder" into Google's search engine. But her guilty
verdict that same week did not dissuade Weinstein
from trying to have similar computer searches barred
from Neil Entwistle's trial. He called the evidence investigators seized "fruits of the poisonous tree."

Weinstein failed to mention in the brief that on the
days that the police had searched the Entwistles'
home looking for the missing family, there was no
way Neil could have given permission—he had already fled the country. The memorandum also didn't
mention that Entwistle had not answered any of the
phone calls placed to his cell by Rachel's mom, or the
cops, or anyone else who tried to reach him that day.

Still, Middlesex Superior Court Judge Diane Kottmyer wanted to hear oral arguments from Weinstein and Assistant District Attorney Michael Fabbri on whether or not the Constitution was violated when police searched the house.

The first person to take the stand in that hearing was Hopkinton Police Sergeant Charles Wallace, a lithely built, bald and bespectacled veteran cop who had been with the department for twenty-one years and had worked overseeing the detective squad for seven. He was the sergeant sitting at the desk when Priscilla Matterazzo had first called the Hopkinton police station looking for help finding her daughter's family.

"She said she went to the house and found no one home," Wallace said on the stand under questioning from Michael Fabbri. "She told me that her daughter had a dinner engagement with family friends that she did not keep.

"She found this very unusual. She is very close to her daughter. If her [Rachel's] plans changed suddenly, she would have let her mother know about it.

"She told me that the shades in the house were pulled down. There was a light in the hallway near Neil's office. She could hear the dog barking inside. I told her we would go to the house and check and see what we could find and get back to her."

Wallace described calling Detective Sutton and asking him to conduct the well-being search, telling him, "We have a young couple that recently moved into town that are unaccounted for. Her mother said this is out of the norm for her daughter."

As Sutton drove to the house, Wallace put out a general broadcast over the radio for the missing family's vehicle, a white BMW SUV. No hits came back.

Then Weinstein began questioning the veteran cop. Wearing a black suit and his trademark cowboy boots, he barked remarks more than real inquiries, leading some spectators to roll their eyes at him.

"The actions of the police have come under some scrutiny?" Weinstein asked the sergeant.

"Well, yes," Wallace said, carefully.

"Did you have any conversation about this with fellow officers? What officers failed to do? What officers failed to see?"

Wallace said he thought he may have talked to the state police investigators about it.

"She wasn't shouting, the mother? She didn't sound hysterical?" Weinstein asked.

"No, I wouldn't classify it as hysterical. I would say she was very concerned."

Weinstein asked the sergeant how he'd dispatched Priscilla Matterazzo's call.

"I asked him to assistant on a persons check, to go to the house and see what he could do," Wallace answered.

Weinstein abruptly asked the judge for permission to play a recording of the call Priscilla Matterazzo had made to the Hopkinton police. After a long delay for technical difficulties because Weinstein could not get the CD-ROM containing the call to play on his personal laptop, the worried mom's voice came into the courtroom.

"I can't reach my daughter. I can't reach them by

cell phone. It's really no big deal, but she just moved in a couple of days ago.

"She was supposed to be home for dinner with her girlfriend Joanna, but she wasn't there.

"I was there today, and no one was there. I last spoke to her on Thursday, everything was fine then. I went to the house. I could hear the dog barking. There was a light on in the hallway. Clothing out on the deck.

"She's the type of girl who calls me every single day."

Wallace is then heard on the recording saying, "We'll send someone up there and we'll check it out, and I'll give you a call back to make sure you haven't heard anything. All right?"

"Thank you," Priscilla said before hanging up.

But it was the testimony that came from Hopkinton Police Sergeant Michael Sutton that would prompt several of the spectators with silk roses pinned to their chests to begin to sob uncontrollably.

CHAPTER 21

"IT WAS A COLD night," Sergeant Michael Sutton remembered about the first time he traveled in a marked Hopkinton police cruiser to the cul-de-sac of new estates on Cubs Path after receiving a radio transmission from Wallace back at the base.

Sutton spoke in clipped sentences with a thick Massachusetts accent. He sported a cop's mustache and wore his graying black hair cropped close to his head. Clearly a former military guy, there was no way Sutton was going to let a weasel lawyer like Elliot Weinstein rattle him on the stand.

"I was informed that relatives of people in the house were concerned for their well-being. They had recently moved to the house and there was a missing woman, husband and infant child," he said, adding that he'd arrived at the house "no more than seven minutes" after receiving the transmission, pulling the cruiser into the empty driveway.

"I was the first one there," he said. "I approached the two people standing in front of the house. One was Joanna Gately. She told me that she had a dinner engagement, and she arrived there at seven p.m. She was unable to raise anyone in the house. She appeared very anxious, very nervous. I decided to try and gain entrance to the house."

Sutton described walking around the entire perimeter of 6 Cubs Path, peering in the windows, pulling on doorknobs to see if anything would pop open, but found no unlocked entry points. He too, heard Sally barking at the noise outside the house. He checked the front door and saw that the deadbolt was not engaged.

"We decided to break in," Sutton said. "Using a plastic card, I was able to slip the lock attached to the doorknob.

"I entered into the foyer, the kitchen and the dining room. Various lights were on. The TV was on in the living room. The dog was barking. It appeared no one was home."

By then another cop, Aaron O'Neil, had arrived, and begun searching the basement.

"I went to the second floor. I could hear the sound of a radio in a baby's room, but there was no baby inside. I looked into the master bedroom. I noticed there was not a lot of furniture, and it was a large room. It appeared no one was in the room. I returned to the foyer, and Officer O'Neil told me nobody was in the garage, and there was no vehicle parked in the garage.

"Joanna Gately was on the front steps. She asked me if she could let the dog out, and I let her. She retrieved the dog and brought it outside. She asked to leave a note, and she wrote one and left it on the table in the kitchen.

"I noticed a stack of open mail, a bill from BMW. I picked it up for the sole purpose of the Vehicle Identification Number. Officer O'Neil turned on a digital camera and saw that no pictures had been taken for the last two days.

"Ms. Gately asked if she could stay in the house. I said no, and we all left. I re-secured the front door and did not turn anything off. Gately was speaking to Mrs. Matterazzo on a cell phone, and she handed it to me.

"She sounded upset. She was concerned with locating her daughter's family. I told her it did not appear that there was a carbon monoxide poisoning incident, and told her that I ran the vehicle identification number and called the hospitals, and there was no bad news there."

As Sutton climbed back behind the wheel of the cruiser, he called out to Gately, who told him she was not leaving until Rachel came home. "If you hear from them, let me know, because until then, we will be looking," Sutton remembered replying.

Then he went back on patrol, never for even a second thinking that he would be back the next night to conduct the same search—though with a very different result. His description was too much for many of the people in the courtroom.

Sutton had received a call from the stationhouse telling him that the Matterazzos had been there to file a missing persons report. By then, Joe Flaherty had called the state police, and there was pressure from the very top of the department to find the Entwistle family. This time, Sutton would not need to break into the house with his credit card. Joanna Gately had obtained the garage code from a neighbor and had passed it along to police.

"We noticed a slight foul odor," Sutton said. "It was unpleasant.

"We followed the odor up the stairs to the second floor where it started to get stronger. We started walking towards the master bedroom where it got stronger still," he said.

Then, the rancid stench had hit him and Detective Scott vanRaalten in the face.

The sound of sniffling could be heard in the courtroom as several of the women present began to cry.

"It was a strong foul odor like a baby's diaper. I looked into the master bedroom and in the center of the bed was a pile of blankets. I noticed eyeglasses and a watch on the floor next to the bed.

"I lifted the comforter and I saw a foot," he said. "I replaced it and called to the detective. I said, 'Boy, you've got to see this.' "

Detective vanRaalten came to the bed and saw the foot. He moved to the headboard side and together the men lifted the comforter. The nightlight next to the king-size bed cast the crime scene in an eerie yellow glow.

"The first thing I saw was a baby's face. It was bruised. The baby had been dead for some time. The first thing I thought was that the baby had been beaten, because of the bruising," Sutton said. "There were obvious signs of death present."

Sutton then said that the baby was the little girl seen in pictures hanging throughout 6 Cubs Path.

"There were a lot of photographs around that house," he mused.

The cops remembered that there was a husband living there too, and he was listed on the missing persons report. As vanRaalten searched the house, Sutton stared at the baby. "Her face was bruised, mottled. The baby had been beaten. Beaten."

Weinstein began to question Sutton—especially on what had merited breaking into the Entwistle house to begin with.

"There was nothing unusual about lights being on in the house, was there?" he asked.

"Not necessarily," Sutton answered.

"Isn't it true that the women [Joanna Gately and her sister] arrived over two hours late for a dinner date, rings the doorbell and finds no one at home?" Weinstein asked. "There was no blood. No signs of emergency in the house, but you looked through paperwork? And then, on the second visit, you find two dead bodies upstairs?"

"Yes," was all Sutton had to say.

Weinstein was unable to cast too much doubt on the police officers' actions during the hearing. The Entwistle family had clearly not taken a last-minute vacation that they did not tell anyone about. Sally was in her cage; there was water run in the bathtub; there were unwashed dishes on the kitchen counter; the television was left on. Judging from the description of Rachel Entwistle, she did not seem to be the type to take off for a trip while leaving her house in a big mess.

Truth be told, the court hearing did not seem to

sway anyone to Weinstein's side of the argument. It would be very hard for anyone to shake the image of two cops lifting a white down comforter up to find the bodies of a young mother and her baby daughter stiff and discolored, lying in each other's arms.

That is exactly the effect that Assistant District Attorney Michael Fabbri was hoping the officers' testimony would have during the oral arguments to admit the evidence seized as part of the case against Neil Entwistle. He wanted everyone to remember how grisly the crime had been. He wanted to hammer home the point that cops had gone into the house at the urging of Rachel Entwistle's panicky mom. Middlesex County District Attorney Gerry Leone had signed his own memorandum, which had been filed with the judge days before the hearing, asking that Weinstein's request be denied

> *because (1) the two entries by police into the home were lawful under the community caretaking functions of the police; (2) entry into the home and discovery of the victims' bodies were inevitable; and (3) the defendant abandoned the Hopkinton home he was renting and had lived in for only one week when he flew to England with a one-way ticket and carrying no luggage.*

The memorandum described the demeanors of Ms. Gately as "very distressed," and stated that she was showing "a high level of anxiety about the situation."

Besides, the memorandum went on to state, the cops did receive subsequent search warrants from the Framingham District Court on January 23 and January

25, 2006, warrants that were issued based on Trooper Banks' affidavit:

Seven additional search warrants [were] issued from [the same] court between January 27, 2006 and February 8, 2006, authorizing forensic analyses of data stored electronically on computer equipment previously seized pursuant to warrant. Two additional warrants issued (from Palo Alto, California and Santa Clara, California) for electronic mail documents connected with Neil Entwistle's Adult Friend Finder account and electronic mail documents from Rachel Entwistle's Hotmail account.

Prosecutors argued that "Local police officers are charged with 'community caretaking functions, totally divorced from the detection, investigation, or acquisition of evidence relating to the violation of a criminal statute.'" The prosecution went on to list a slew of cases where searches were deemed legal—even without a warrant—if there is an

objectively reasonable basis for believing that the safety of an individual or the public is jeopardized . . . Because such a situation involves an entry based on an emergency and not for criminal investigative purposes, probable cause is not required to enter.

So, prosecutors argued, there was a myriad of factors involved in the first two searches, the ones conducted without a warrant that justified their entry. There had been a hysterical mother at the Hopkinton police station begging for help, a call that had come from a well-respected retired homicide investigator urging the cops to take the missing persons report seriously, and a young couple, with a new baby, who were unfamiliar with their new home.

> *Not only was it reasonable for the Hopkinton officers to enter the home, but the public would expect as much.*
>
> *The Entwistles disappeared suddenly, without notice, and without explanation. The people closest to them were highly alarmed and essentially begged police to help them figure out what happened to them. It was wholly out of character for Rachel not to have contact with her mother for two days, and similarly out of character for Rachel to desert the Gatelys, who were invited for dinner with the Entwistles on the evening of Saturday, January 21, 2006. Both Mrs. Mattarrazzo [sic] and Ms. Gately had tried to reach the family by calling Rachel, knocking on the door, and ringing the bell, to no avail.*

The prosecution described Sutton and vanRaalten going house to house on Cubs Path, curious if anyone had seen the couple. They had heard answers similar to the ones given to reporters the night of the murder. Neighbors had seen moving vans. They'd spotted Rachel pushing a baby stroller, Neil collecting mail. Nothing out of the ordinary was reported. Then there

was the second search inside the home, after Joanna
Gately had managed to wrangle the security code out
of a neighbor.

> *Immediately upon this second entry, Sergeant
> Sutton detected the odor and followed it directly
> to the master bedroom. . . . Although there was a
> delay of almost an entire day between the first
> and second entries into the house, the Entwistles'
> friends and family had become increasingly con-
> cerned regarding their continued disappearance,
> and Sergeant Sutton reasonably decided to
> check the home again while the missing persons
> reports were being completed. . . . After discov-
> ering Rachel and Lillian Entwistles' bodies, the
> police cursorily inspected the home for Neil En-
> twistle, who still had not been located. The Hop-
> kinton police acted reasonably in all respects.*

The dog could be heard barking inside, yet fresh
ice and snow had yet to be removed from the walk-
way outside. The mail was certain to overflow and the
odor would have eventually enveloped the entire
neighborhood.

> *Ultimately, the bodies of the victims would have
> been discovered, either by police or by civilians,
> and a murder investigation would have fol-
> lowed.*

But it was the final argument in the prosecution's
brief that really made the point:

The defendant abandoned the Hopkinton home he had rented and resided in for one week when he returned to his native country via a one-way ticket.

In addition, the defendant showed no subjective expectation of privacy in the home because he abandoned it when he left his dead wife and daughter in the home and flew across the Atlantic to England. . . . the defendant's intent not to return to the home was apparent from the fact that he bought a one-way ticket to England, where he was still a citizen. . . .

His actions summed up one presumption on the part of investigators.

Neil Entwistle, the argument went, had abandoned his Fourth Amendment rights to privacy when he fled the country. He wasn't even a United States citizen.

With that, Assistant District Attorney Fabbri put his final witness, Detective Scott vanRaalten, on the stand for the day to argue that every single move the Hopkinton police had made in search of the Entwistle family was appropriate and necessary. He, too, described pulling into Cubs Path, "a typical American neighborhood," entering the house and being met with a God-awful smell.

"The sergeant told me, 'That smell wasn't here last night,'" the detective said. "It was really awful, the smell. Like dirty diapers."

He was not particularly seasoned in homicide investigations. In fact, he had never had one before the Entwistle case. But when Sergeant Sutton pulled up the white comforter and vanRaalten spotted Rachel's foot under the sheet, the detective was shaken.

"There were obvious signs of death. Discoloration of the foot," he said of finding Rachel's corpse. That was enough to rattle vanRaalten, but what he saw next would haunt him for the rest of his life.

"There was a small child in her mother's arms . . ." VanRaalten's voice trailed off. "There was something coming out of her mouth. Discoloration on her face. Bruises. Blood coming out of her mouth and nose."

Weinstein had no further questions and the hearing ended.

Outside the courtroom it was Weinstein's turn to be peppered with questions, only these came from the press. A television reporter embraced him as he came out of the courtroom, and two scribes from the daily newspapers rolled their eyes.

The first question fired was, "Is your client on medication?"

Weinstein responded with a cold stare and then ignored the journalist completely, turning his attention back to the television reporter with the heavily made-up face.

"Elliot," she said, "tell us what happened in court today."

Weinstein repeated his argument that the search was illegal and that the law "does not permit law enforcement to enter a private home because someone asked them to.

"There were no signs of emergency, no signs of problem. There is no case law to support their brief. Most law enforcement would not enter a home without valid reasons. The ends do not justify the means."

But that's exactly what investigators thought about the actions Neil Entwistle was accused of—shooting a baby in the belly because you weren't getting enough sex and you didn't have enough money. That end for Rachel and Lilly Entwistle certainly was unjustified.

CHAPTER 22

AS GERRY LEONE AND his prosecution team grew increasingly worried with each passing week that Middlesex Superior Court Judge Diane Kottmyer did not issue a decision as to whether the evidence from the search of the Entwistle home was in fact legal, and would be admissible during Neil's trial, they suddenly had a much larger problem on their hands.

The *Boston Globe* had uncovered a scandal in the State Police Crime Lab, which was responsible for processing and testing DNA samples for every major incident of violence that occurred in Massachusetts—including the Entwistle case. It seemed that a longtime scientist who'd acted as the administrator of the DNA database had mishandled test results in about two dozen sexual assault cases—blunders that allowed rapists linked to unsolved attacks to remain free. Robert Pino, considered the state's DNA expert, was suspended from his duties and then fired from the State Crime Lab after failing to report to prosecutors that DNA had linked twenty-one men to unsolved rapes before the statute of limitations on the crime ran out. Within weeks of Elliot Weinstein's argument that the evidence should be tossed from his client's murder trial, he now actually had something he could seize upon that could cast doubt on Neil Entwistle's guilt.

Serious questions were being raised about the validity of the DNA that had been recovered on the handle of Joseph Matterazzo's .22-caliber handgun. Attorneys began to petition that the DNA results be thrown out.

Leone himself had five unsolved rape cases dating back fifteen to twenty years that would never see justice, even though attackers had been identified through their DNA. He said he would "locate and notify each of the victims" of the outrageous mistakes. Leone also said that his office was trying to find loopholes to extend the statute of limitations for the amount of time that a defendant was not living in Massachusetts—but that was a stretch.

Elliot Weinstein was heard saying that the new information emerging about DNA mismanagement "calls into question the reliability, trustworthiness and integrity" of all the work conducted in the State Police Crime Lab.

Including what Weinstein referred to as the "so-called" match that linked Neil Entwistle to the murder weapon used to kill Rachel and Lillian.

The Dasani water bottle found in the cup holder should have been enough, Elliot Weinstein had argued in his legal brief just months before the uproar broke out. Any other collection of Neil Entwistle's DNA—as the government wanted—would be nothing more than a violation of his civil rights.

That argument was contained in a brief Weinstein filed in October 2006, ten months after Rachel's brain matter had been found splattered on the muzzle end—and Neil Entwistle's DNA was found on the grip—of a .22-caliber gun that belonged to her stepfather. It was written after the Middlesex County District Attorney's office petitioned a judge to order that investigators be allowed to collect a sample of DNA from the inside of Neil Entwistle's cheek—infuriating Weinstein, who called the move an intrusion on his client's time.

After all, Neil was very busy reading the Bible and avoiding Eben Howard at the Middlesex lockup. He had no time for dealing with meddlesome cops. Besides, Weinstein argued, the crime lab's own forensic scientist had declared that the DNA conclusions of a laboratory analysis months earlier of the mixture on the swab from the revolver matched Rachel Entwistle as the "major female profile"—and concluded that Neil Entwistle "could have been the potential contributor" of the DNA on the barrel of the gun. Those matches were made from saliva found on Neil's Dasani bottle and from a sample Rachel's family voluntarily gave investigators.

Apparently choosing his words carefully to make sure he in no way acknowledged a belief that the DNA was a match, but only a theory that state prosecutors were using to prove their case, Weinstein wrote:

The repeated use of these unreliable DNA analysis results clearly violate Mr. Entwistle's right to due process of law and fair trial as guaranteed by the Fifth and Sixth Amendments to the United States Constitution . . .

As an initial observation, the Commonwealth has conducted scientific DNA testing and comparison analysis, and has reported results which, in the Commonwealth's choice of language, show a match between Neil Entwistle's DNA and DNA on various evidentiary items including what the Commonwealth believes to be the murder weapon—a .22 caliber revolver. Based on the assertions disseminated by the Commonwealth, there is no need to obtain a buccal swab from Mr. Entwistle and the Commonwealth's motion should be denied.

It was ironic however that the words of Gwen Pino, supervisor of the Massachusetts State Police Crime Laboratory, would be used by Entwistle's attorney to prove his point. That same supervisor's husband, Robert, would be fired months later by the Governor of Massachusetts for incompetence. And in further proof that the Massachusetts law enforcement community is a small one, Gwen Pino's findings on another rape case had also repeatedly been called into question. But before it was exposed that DNA had been mishandled in the crime lab, Gwen Pino was quoted in court filings in the Entwistle case, saying, "in order for DNA analysis to be reliable, a DNA standard sample should be taken directly from a suspect in accordance with laboratory police guidelines."

Indeed, Weinstein noted.

In other words, the Commonwealth is asserting that it has previously obtained DNA comparison results, that it has relied upon those results and disseminated those results in various forums but now acknowledges those results are not reliable.

Of course, the attorney had no idea how true those words would become as he wrote his argument, ticking off the "various forums" that the DNA results were cited in by Middlesex County prosecutors.

1. *Request for provisional arrest warrant. . . .*
2. *Further statement of Facts In Support of Extradition Request. . . .*
3. *February 8, 2006 Hopkinton Police Sergeant Joseph Bennet affidavit in support of application for criminal complaint submitted for both complaint and arrest warrant. . . .*
4. *March 29, 2006 DNA-STR Report of Department of State Police Crime. Laboratory Analyst Laura Bryant: "The DNA profile obtained from the swab of revolver—R52151—gripped area of handle is a mixture of DNA from at least two individuals. Neil Entwistle . . . matched the major male profile in this DNA mixture.*

   The DNA profile obtained from the swab of revolver . . . barrel is a mixture of DNA from at least two individuals . . . Neil Entwistle is included as a potential contributor of the minor profile in this mixture." . . .

5. *March, 2006 Commonwealth's statement of the case filed in this court. . . .*
6. *September, 2006 Massachusetts State Trooper Michael Banks affidavit submitted in support of Commonwealth's motion for buccal swab. . . .*

To make matters worse, Weinstein argued, the DNA results had been cited by virtually every news medium available—television, newspapers, magazines and the Internet—making it impossible for Neil Entwistle to find a jury of his peers not tainted by the knowledge that investigators had linked him to the murder weapon using science, not just theory. He cited twenty-three reports that repeated prosecutors' assertions that Entwistle was in fact guilty of killing his wife and child, from Nancy Grace's discussions of the case on CNN, Greta Van Susteren's theories on Fox News Network, and headlines in the *Boston Herald* and *Globe*, as well as local TV coverage. There were headlines like "Cops: The husband did it; Saying they've got the gun, DNA evidence and a motive, police nab Neil Entwistle for the brutal murder of his wife, Rachel, and 9-month-old daughter Lillian," in *People* magazine.

He went on to write that prosecutors were trying to

avoid being bound by unreliable DNA evidentiary conclusions, and its own reporting of these unreliable results, by initiating a new round of forensic DNA comparison analysis with a controlled sample obtained from Mr. Entwistle. This Court should deny this request.

Further, this Court should conclude that the repeated dissemination of the now recognized unreliable DNA conclusions denies Mr. Entwistle his basic and fundamental constitutional right to due process of law.

But there was a caveat included at the end of the legal brief that said *if* a judge were to allow for the government to obtain a buccal swab from Neil Entwistle, there had to be stipulations, seven, in fact:

1. *The Commonwealth should acknowledge and agree that any prior reporting of a DNA match between Mr. Entwistle's DNA and any physical or biological evidence was unreliable;*
2. *The Commonwealth will not attempt to take a buccal swab from Mr. Entwistle until he and his counsel have had the opportunity to consult with a qualified expert regarding the proper procedure for collection of a buccal swab;*
3. *Mr. Entwistle's counsel and, at their election, a qualified expert will be present;*
4. *The Commonwealth will provide defense counsel with the name and qualifications of the person designated to take the buccal swab at least 14 days prior to the date agreed upon for taking said swab so as to permit, if defense counsel chooses, a pre-swab challenge to the designee's qualifications;*
5. *As minimal a sample as necessary shall be taken, so as to cause minimum inconvenience to Mr. Entwistle;*

6. *No questioning of any kind is to be directed at Mr. Entwistle;*
7. *The parties shall make reasonable effort to complete taking the buccal swab within 30 days of the date of the order of the court.*

It was a smart move on Weinstein's part to lay down his version of the law when it came to collecting the DNA swab, because, as he might have guessed before he even wrote the eight-page brief, Superior Court Justice Peter Lauriat decided in favor of the government and ordered that Neil Entwistle submit to the test. In his ruling, he said:

> *This Court finds that the testing is necessary evidence for both the Commonwealth and the Defense. According, the Court is herby ORDERS that the Massachusetts State Police Crime Lab be permitted to conduct exhaustive testing on the samples in question, provided that an expert for the defendant be present, or the defendant waives the expert's presence.*

Lauriat also agreed to allow investigators to study the ammo boxes, a gun lock and the trigger, hammer and chamber of the murder weapon.

Lauriat signed his order on October 5, 2006. Months later, every DNA test that had been conducted in that laboratory was being called into question. The FBI had swarmed the lab with investigators. An expensive independent audit was being conducted. The governor of the state was publicly pissed.

The mishandling of DNA was recounted in headlines in the daily newspapers with increasing frequency. Middlesex County District Attorney Gerry Leone found himself in the position of defending the DNA collected from Neil Entwistle, telling cops and reporters, "We are confident that the DNA will pass muster."

And while Weinstein might have lost his first battle against the DNA evidence that would in all likelihood be used at Neil Entwistle's trial, it was still possible that he could win the war.

By late July 2007, it became official that the State Police Crime Lab debacle—which had widened by now to include charges that investigators had failed to test 16,000 crime-scene samples for DNA matches—could cause a serious delay in the trial of Neil Entwistle. It had been more than a year-and-a-half since the bodies of Rachel and Lillian had been found, but forensic evidence taken from their home had not been processed. And even if it had, there was no doubt that Neil's lawyers would want those results verified by an independent lab, given how unreliable the crime lab had proven to be.

That same month, a federal judge, Nancy Gertner, awarded the country's largest settlement—a staggering $101.7 million—to two men, and the families of two others, who she said had been framed for murder by the New England FBI office thirty-three years earlier. Two of the men, Louis Greco and Henry Tameleo, had died behind bars. The other two, Joseph Salvati and Peter Limone, grew old behind bars and were freed after spending the bulk of their lives in prison. "FBI officials up the line allowed their employees to break laws, violate rules and ruin lives," Gertner said as she ordered the government to pay the four innocent men who had sued, as many people in the courtroom applauded.

The case meant a lot more than money, though. Once again, the integrity of the Boston FBI office—which had been rife with scandals, including one that would provide the basis for the Oscar-winning movie *The Departed*—was being publicly exposed. No one in the FBI was held accountable for the blatant disregard for the law, and the willful misconduct of the agents involved in sending the four innocent men to prison. Once again, many people in Massachusetts, including potential jurors who would decide Neil Entwistle's fate, felt as if the government could not be trusted, and would in fact lie to garner a conviction in a high-profile murder case.

Gerry Leone would staunchly deny that the State Police Crime Lab scandal would cause a delay in the prosecution of Neil Entwistle, saying that the trial would still be held in October 2007 as planned. But even if it did go forward, it was very possible that the twelve jurors and the alternate picked in the case would remember the headlines from shoddy investigative work, shady FBI agents and total forensic incompetence.

CHAPTER 23

IF NEIL ENTWISTLE HAD a window in his cell on Memorial Day in 2007, he would have been able to look out and see the Charles River in Boston, the towering Prudential Center and the skyline of Boston at its most attractive time: the start of summer. But there was no window, and it was unlikely that Entwistle would be gazing at the skyline of any city—whether in Massachusetts or his native England—any time soon.

A year-and-a-half after his wife and daughter had been murdered, Neil remained in the same cell that had held him ever since that April day when he was surrounded on the Tube in London by British police. He still had an ever-present guard by his cell to prevent him from committing suicide. like John C. Salvi III, the anti-abortion zealot who went on a shooting rampage, killing two clinic employees and wounding five others on December 20, 1994. He shot one victim, Lee Ann Nichols, ten times as she begged for her life screeching: "This is what you get! You should pray the rosary!" During his sentencing, Salvi told a judge he wanted to receive the death penalty, which was not an option in Massachusetts.

So, after serving two years of his life sentence, Salvi swallowed a sock, tightly wound a trash bag around his head, and took his own life in his cell at Walpole, the prison that houses the state's most violent convicts. (It is now called MCI–Cedar Junction.) The Department of Correction could ill-afford a dramatic suicide from a high-profile inmate such as Entwistle, and guards were especially wary of him because of the depressed musings found in his cell in the letter to Yvonne and Clifford Entwistle after a judge told him he could not go home to England and spend the Christmas holidays with them.

Elliot Weinstein was still fighting on Neil Entwistle's behalf, but he was also busy with his latest client: a violent pimp who was accused of running a prostitution ring that kidnapped young girls and forced them into sex at secret brothels up and down the East Coast. Six men were arrested in all, but Weinstein's client, Eddie "Young Indian" Jones, a 24-year-old from Roxbury, the bloodiest neighborhood in Boston, was especially brutal. He was charged with booting a teenage girl in the face with his Timberland boots, knocking out of all of her teeth, after he'd caught her talking on a cell phone with another man. After he disfigured her, prosecutors said, he gave her back to another pimp because she could not make him any money. Another hero to add to Elliot Weinstein's rogues' gallery of clients.

At this point, the media throngs that had followed Neil Entwistle's every move on both sides of the Atlantic had dispersed. There was rarely any mention of the case in the papers. The defense and the prosecution were still waiting for the judge to decide whether or not to admit the DNA evidence collected from the Dasani bottle, or the buccal swab scraped against the inside of his cheek, to be presented. Also, the judge had yet to render a decision about whether to allow the searches made in Entwistle's house and the family's BMW SUV, or the statements he'd made to police from England. Weinstein continued to try to have all of the evidence collected in those searches and interviews thrown out.

A memorial scholarship that had been set up in honor of Rachel for students at Silver Lake Regional High School in Kingston, did not use her married name. Fundraisers, or "times" as they were called in Massachusetts, continued to be held on the South Shore to raise money for the Rachel Souza Memorial Scholarship Fund. If anyone attending the parties mentioned her husband, it was in hushed tones so no one would overhear. An executive of the Sovereign Bank, which started the fund with a donation of $1,000 within weeks of the murders, announced: "We join with the Souza family in their desire to see something positive emerge from the overwhelming tragedy of losing a beloved daughter and granddaughter." Priscilla and her son continued to work on setting a list of criteria for students who wanted to apply for the scholarship that would best exemplify Rachel: her love of Henry David Thoreau, her passion for drama, and her love of the outdoors.

Strangers continued to post comments and photographs on a web page set up in memory of Rachel and

Lillian Rose by an anonymous mourner. There was no mention of Neil by name anywhere on the site—not in the loving comments about the mother and baby, not in the bios, not even in the history of the case. And Neil did not appear in a single picture. As with the obituaries that appeared in local papers, no one wanted to remember Neil Entwistle. It was as though he had been erased from the family's history.

Unfortunately for Priscilla Matterazzo, it would be impossible to wipe his memory completely from her mind. Every time she sat at the kitchen table, she would glance over at the chair where Neil had sat across from her when he and Rachel first arrived in the country, as the two shared a cup of coffee. In retrospect, his words—and even the way he said them—seemed somewhat whiny and eerily frightening at the same time: "Rachel was always more family-oriented than I was."

On the memorial website, a poem was posted alongside a digital flickering candle, much like the one that had been lit at the baby's christening, reminding all present of the loving hand of God.

> *When tomorrow starts without me,*
> *And I'm not there to see,*
> *If the sun should rise and find your eyes*
> *All filled with tears for me,*
>
> *I wish so much you wouldn't cry*
> *The way you did today,*
> *While thinking of the many things,*
> *We didn't get to say.*

I know how much you love me,
As much as I love you,
And each time that you think of me,
I know you'll miss me too.

If I could re-live yesterday
Just even for a while,
I'd say good-bye and kiss you
And maybe see you smile.

So when tomorrow starts without me,
Don't think we're far apart,
For every time you think of me,
I'm right here, in your heart.

The site's visitors' book was filled with comments that began days after the murders in January 2006 and continued into Mother's Day 2007. Some of the comments were posted by former students in Redditch: "there aren't words to describe what you two meant to me," wrote one girl named Ellie. "We miss you forever. all my love. xxxxxx." Ellie also had a MySpace page where she posted memories of "Enty" and how much her American drama teacher influenced her life. There were other messages from students as well. One young man named Hev Williams paid tribute to a "lovely woman with not a bad bone in her body," and a teenage girl named Laura Mogg wrote, "She was my theatre studies teacher for three years and she was absolutely wonderful." But another English student named Adam Burgess described Rachel perfectly: "She was an awesome teacher and she really helped me get good grades but, yes above all, she was one of the nicest people ever."

On April 9, 2007, on what would have been Lillian Rose Entwistle's second birthday, a friend named Michelle posted: "Happy Birthday 2nd Birthday Sweet Lillian!! I'm sure you and your mommy are spending a fun day together wishing for smiles as you watch over your family and friends who miss you terribly!" One simply read like this: "Any murder is wrong, but to murder an innocent baby and her mother is beyond reason." What was sad was that even the site www.neilentwistle.com was filled with pictures of Rachel and Lillian, posted in memory along with a guest book where strangers and friends wrote messages of condolence to her "family and students." The owner of the site in Florida had decided to dedicate it to Rachel and Lilly rather than profit from it.

DESPITE THE CEASELESS MOURNING for Rachel's death, financial problems—some of the very financial problems that prosecutors believed had prompted Neil's actions—continued to plague her survivors. Unpaid bills were being sent to her estate, which was being handled by Priscilla Matterazzo. Creditors had filed court papers seeking nearly $9,000 for unpaid credit cards held by MBNA and Citibank. One bill was for $8,121 and the other was $666. Then there were outstanding student loans. The big corporations clearly did not care that Rachel had been cut down before ever being given a chance to pay up, and her mounting debt was now falling on the grieving shoulders of her mother.

Money was also becoming an issue for the owners of the house in Hopkinton. They were trying desperately to unload it. It was still kind of a macabre attraction, with true crime buffs pulling onto the small road to catch a glimpse of the suburban home where such a horrible double murder could take place. No one who knew about its history would rent it, and no Realtor would dare try to show it without divulging its tragic history. The owners had no choice but to put it on the market during the Massachusetts housing slump.

A local agent wrote up an advertisement that was sent to real estate listings on the Internet and in newspapers highlighting the obvious features of the 2,432-square-foot house:

> *Spacious Colonial situated on a cul-de-sac in a desirable family neighborhood: ** Four bedrooms, 3½ baths; eat-in kitchen with oak cabinets, built-in desk and pantry; Family room with cathedral ceiling and masonry fireplace; Enclosed porch off the kitchen; Finished walk-out basement with family room/playroom; Office with full bath; Oversize patio area with 8-person hot tub; Two car garage; Asphalt, shingle roof; Well water and septic system; Central air; Central oil heat; Just minutes to Mass Pike, Route 495, and the commuter rail.*

All that, and the yard stretched back nearly an acre. Of course, the ad made no mention that a specialized crime-scene cleanup team had been hired to go into the house and wipe out the smell of death. The cleaners wore hazmat suits as they scrubbed at splatters of brain matter or blood. There was also the fingerprint dust and other remnants left behind by forensic scientists from the State Police Crime Lab who had thoroughly processed every square inch of the room. To make it even more difficult for the house's owners to get out from under, it had been made clear to them that once Neil Entwistle was brought to trial, it was very likely that jurors would be brought to the house for a walk-through. "It's standard procedure to allow a jury to tour the crime scene. If the house was sold, we would make arrangements for it to happen with the new owners," Corey Welford, a spokesman for the Office of the Middlesex District Attorney, explained. "We would do it in any case, with deference to the owners."

If any prospective buyers showed interest, they could be spooked by the knowledge that thirteen strangers, along with defense attorneys and prosecutors, could be traipsing through the master bedroom to envision the bloodletting that had taken place there. The murders could even be reenacted. Furniture could be moved into position to replicate the spot where Rachel and Lillian were lying when they were shot.

The house was on the market for $549,900—a lowball figure on the pricey cul-de-sac—but there was never a lot of interest shown. In fact, the *Boston Herald* conducted an online poll of its readers to see how many would buy the house in spite of the terrible crime that had taken place inside, and more than seventy percent responded that there was no way in hell. It was likely to be haunted, many believed, and no amount of burnt sage could cast out its negative energy. Months later, the price was dropped nearly $50,000, but still the house remained on the market.

The owners did hold out hope. After all, in nearby Framingham, a couple had bought the house of Richard Rosenthal, the man who'd killed his wife after she burned the ziti she was cooking for dinner, and then impaled her organs on a stake in the back yard in 1995. Even the house in Holliston where Kenneth Seguin had hacked his wife and children to death in 1992 was purchased by new owners. One of them, Tom Driscoll, would tell a reporter, "I think our feeling was, yes, there had been a tragedy here, but there was as much we could do to redeem the house by putting together the loving household we tried to put together here." The owners of 6 Cubs Path were hoping people like Driscoll would tour their house. For now it seemed there would be no new owners, at least as long as people remained unsettled by the tragedy that had unfolded inside.

SALLY, THE BASSETT HOUND Neil Entwistle had left caged in the house when he fled the country, settled into a new life in Carver with the Matterazzos. Priscilla and Joe had taken her home with them from the Hopkinton police station on the day they filed the missing persons report with Joanna Gately and her sister caring for Sally outside. Even if they didn't love her, the Matterazzos would have taken Sally in. After all, it was her incessant bark that had alerted Rachel's friends that something was amiss inside the house. If not for Sally, Hopkinton police might have taken even longer to realize that something was indeed very wrong on that freezing night in 2006.

THE NEIL ENTWISTLE CASE once again prompted debate about reinstating capital punishment in Massachusetts. Many felt the death penalty should be reinstated, especially when confronted with the shooting deaths of an innocent woman and an infant. But given that it is a largely Democratic state with liberal judges who are appointed to the bench by liberal governors, it is unlikely that would happen any time soon. Neil Entwistle had already indicated with his hinted threats of suicide that he would rather die than go on with life in prison. He may have welcomed a death sentence, especially when he considered spending the rest of his years in a high-security prison like MCI–Cedar Junction, one of the most dangerous in the country.

Every con in the system, and most cops, still refer to the prison by its old name, Walpole. In the 1970s there was a group of lifers imprisoned there who called themselves "the Death Squad," convicted killers who essentially had nothing to lose and everything to gain by keeping up their reputations behind the wall as scary, violent people. The Death Squad made it its mission to exterminate prisoners convicted of sex crimes and violence against children, leading to a series of baffling and unsolved murders committed at the hands of convicts. Mysteriously, there were never any witnesses to the homicides—not even guards. Some people believed that the guards were somehow complicit. One pedophile was decapitated; his head was found in the jailhouse laundry.

But those days were long gone. Now anyone convicted of sex crimes against children was housed at a prison for the sexually dangerous, so as not to be harmed by the general population. Baby killers, however, were another matter entirely. Some went to MCI–Norfolk, where conditions were lax enough that convicts once started a Lifers Group that hosted Christmas parties and BBQs, until stopped by officials. Most, however, went to Walpole.

Neil Entwistle may have been a big man, but spending more than a year in prison had turned his bearish hulk into congealed flab. Already he was prone to the type of street violence that most of the cons in Walpole had grown up with, and it was very unlikely he would be able to defend himself against any attacks. Cons like Neil Entwistle were often forced to find protection, and in doing so, became the romantic love interests of bigger men in the system. Walpole was filled with hardscrabble neighborhood guys: bank robbers from Charlestown, gang bangers from Dorchester, and drug lords from East Boston. The only fellow lifer Neil Entwistle might be able to befriend at Walpole was Kenneth Seguin. Elliot Weinstein's bid to keep that guy out of jail had failed, and, given the evidence that was mounting against Neil Entwistle—even with the DNA debacle in the State Police Crime Lab—it seemed that the lawyer would be just as unsuccessful in this case.

If Weinstein's defense did not sway a jury, men like Eben Howard would be the very least of Neil's problems.

CHAPTER 24

NEIL ENTWISTLE WAS WEARY. Tired of eating white bread and bologna sandwiches. Tired of the incessant white noise around him, the buzz of electric cell doors, the moans and songs and yells from other prisoners. Tired of the barely concealed scowls of disdain that came from deputy sheriffs. Tired of the tedium, the one hour a day out of his cell. Tired of the lukewarm showers. Tired of the cold steel toilet without a seat. Tired of worrying about encountering someone who was going to kick him in the groin. Tired of the nightmares. Tired of worrying about what his parents thought of him. Tired of the infrequent trips to court where he was glared at by Rachel's family. Tired of Bible stories and romance novels. Tired of the orange jumpsuit he was forced to wear because of his high security threat classification.

Tired of his thumb automatically going to his wedding ring finger and not finding anything there.

He was also filled with regrets. The biggest one being that on the morning of that terrible day when Rachel and Lillian were killed—at least according to what he'd told State Police Trooper Michael Banks—Neil had pulled a sharp blade from the knife block on the family's kitchen counter and contemplated raking it along his wrists, or plunging it into his own heart. Things could be so different now if he had actually gone through with it. The ever-present screaming in his head would have stopped, for one. And at least he could have gone out like a man, instead of having so many people snicker reading Banks' affidavit stating that Neil told him he "considered killing himself, but then put [the knife] down because it would hurt too much."

If Neil Entwistle thought getting rid of his family and fleeing back to his native country would free him of the wreckage of mounting debt and the trappings of a passionless marriage, he was sadly mistaken. The murders were hardly a reprieve, and in retrospect, the discovery of Rachel and Lillian's bloody bodies had presented a set of much bigger problems for him to overcome. But addicts often impulsively act out, looking for the easier, softer way to squelch an uncomfortable situation, without ever thinking of the consequences of their actions until it is much too late. Experts would describe Neil as a classic addict, who exhibited all the signs of a compulsive obsessive disorder. He was full of low self-esteem, but at the same time had a streak of narcissism prompting an observer familiar with the case to remark: "Neil Entwistle doesn't think much of himself, but he's all he ever thinks about."

In addition to the letter that Neil had written to his parents, another one had been obtained by authorities addressed to his lawyer Elliot Weinstein and another attorney assisting him, Stephanie Page. The letter was yet another glimpse into Neil Entwistle's delusions of grandeur, the lofty idea he had of himself—not the least of which was the misconception that the remains of his burned cadaver would be worthy of being sprinkled over Rachel and Lillian's grave. The hand-scrawled letter had just a vague date: December 2006. It was written on long, lined legal paper with a felt-tip pen, the only writing implement he was allowed to possess in the jail. And it was filled with instructions on how he wanted his remains taken care of. The letter was expected to become part of the court record, but remained under seal. It included lines like these:

Dear Elliot and Stephanie,
    I wish to be cremated and if possible have my ashes scattered on Rachel and Lillian's grave.
    Other than this, I do not care unless my parents want half to do with as they see fit.

He then listed as the "only items" he cared about, his wedding ring, photos on his laptop, and certain items he and mentioned in February/March. The letter closed:

    One day my mood was fine. Then it started to darken.
    And if you are reading this, then I guess it got worse.
    I have no other explanation.
                                        Yours Sincerely,
                                        N. Entwistle

He signed the letter with the same loopy *N* and elongated crossed *t* that he had signed court papers with, prompting one law enforcement official who saw it to remark that Neil's handwriting was like "a junior high school girl's." The letter must have been written around the same time he wrote the suicidal farewell letter to his parents, but because the jailers had no authority to read legal mail, in all likelihood, Weinstein became worried about his client and notified the proper channels. The letter became part of the sealed court case. (Officials remained so paranoid about the judge's order not to publicly discuss the case prior to the trial that before a copy of Neil Entwistle's letter to his lawyers was obtained for this book, it was handled by a law enforcement official who wore gloves, wrapped the copy in a paper towel and sealed in a plastic bag so its source could not be traced by fingerprinting. The precautions were a sign that many people saw Entwistle's own words as a sort of admission in the case, and any leaks to the media about the letter could help Weinstein argue that his client's jury pool was completely spoiled.)

There were many ways to interpret Neil Entwistle's words, depending on whether someone believed he was guilty or innocent. Investigators contended, at least among themselves, that the words "One day my mood was fine. Then it started to darken" could point to the days leading up the homicides when Neil was trolling the Internet for sex partners and escort services and using the Google search engine to find ways to kill and methods of committing suicide. Or the night that Rachel was last heard from, when he drove to a local mall and bought $88 worth of candles, believed to be the props for some sort of lascivious encounter. Investigators, were checking the mileage on the BMW to see how far the drove the at night—the last that Rachel Entwistle was heard from alive. After all, Neil Entwistle had spent years in the porn racket, and as any addictive personality knows, it was hard to pull out of the seething cauldron of compulsion whether the obsession of choice was booze, drugs, sex or shopping. In his case, given the photo Neil posted of his fully aroused penis on the Adult FriendFinder website, and his meandering search for prostitutes on the Internet, he was certainly looking for more than "fun in the bedroom." He was looking to fill the hole in his gut, the ceaseless restlessness and unease that had infected him since he was a little boy, leaving him with such a sense of insecurity that he'd told Rachel he was convinced it was his working-class English accent that would prevent him from having a good life. Not a lack of drive or initiative. But his voice.

Is it possible Neil Entwistle's "mood was fine" up until that relapse into sexual debauchery? It would certainly be part of the prosecution's case, along with the photographs that were posted on the Entwistle family website, proof that Neil, Rachel and Lillian were the ideal family unit, straight out of a 1950s television sitcom, with ever-present smiles on the faces of Mommy, Daddy and baby as they posed against perfect suburban backdrops and well-maintained homes. Happiness personified.

But then Neil's carefully constructed house of cards began to topple. The moneyed lifestyle he was boasting about, financed by a secretive job back in England, was a farce. The pricey suburban house they had rented was filled with new furniture they couldn't afford. People were after them—at least verbally, on the Internet—the customers who had been ripped off or conned were mentioning them by name: "Rachel Entwistle is a lying, thieving bitch," one went so far as to write.

Addicts are the ultimate liars, but they also always get caught. It was when the lies began to unravel that everything "started to darken." Finally "it got worse."

Bad enough that he wanted to end it all, some would speculate. Investigators would then argue that Neil Entwistle's only way out was to kill his wife and baby and then himself. Only he was too much of a coward to go through with his compulsive plan. And, as investigators planned to state at his upcoming trial, he wasn't even smart enough to have had a cohesive story in place.

Weinstein would likely argue that the letter was nothing more than additional proof that Neil Entwistle was an innocent man who merely felt wrung out from the ordeal of prison and of judgments made about him before he had been convicted of any crime. Entwistle's suicidal thoughts were probably spawned of the seemingly relentless hatred being spewed at him even from perfect strangers—hence Neil's desire to be cremated, rather than to suffer through the humiliation of having someone yell "Baby killer!" at his corpse, his lawyers would insist. After all, Neil showed nothing but concern for his parents' feelings in the matter, at least according to his letter. He was sentimental enough to want to be buried with his gold wedding band, the ring that was now evidence in the case. He was even gracious enough to thank his attorneys for all their hard work on his behalf. These are not the rambling, incoherent words of a killer, Weinstein might say, but the musings of a wrongly accused man fed up with fighting to prove his innocence when the law says that investigators must shoulder the burden of proving his guilt.

Or maybe his words were just another extension of his con; a weakling's way out. He mentioned the media, and maybe he knew all too well that the letter could be leaked to the press—effectuating influence on a jury pool who, instead of viewing him as a ruthless baby killer, could show empathy for him. They could view him as a disturbed and suicidal sad sack rather than a maniacal, porn-peddling monster. Besides, it was hard to believe that a guy who did not want his "body to be made an example of" was actually suicidal. If someone wanted out of life itself, how could he be concerned with the way his corpse was viewed? If he was an innocent man, why would he care about the "fanfare" that would come with his body being shipped back to England? Like his insistence to State Trooper Michael Banks that the discovery of his murdered wife and baby had nearly driven him to kill himself, the letter to Weinstein might have been another way for Neil Entwistle to try to manipulate the system and land himself back in a cozy hospital room rather than a freezing jail cell.

Even Joe Flaherty said that Rachel's family remained flabbergasted by "the sheer level of Neil's deceit, the unbearable betrayal." If Neil could throw them off course with his lies, it was unlikely that pangs of conscience would prevent him from trying to taint his potential jury pool.

One thing was for sure: Neil Entwistle's letter would definitely be discussed from every angle and by every expert—psychological, legal and even graphological—that the defense and the prosecution could afford. Already one former forensic psychologist had theorized that Entwistle had suffered from catathymia, a condition that involves a steady build-up of anger and frustration leading to a violent explosion. If nothing else, his words provided a small glimpse into Neil Entwistle's mind. Until then, all the public had seen of Neil was his shuffling into courtrooms with a dazed, and probably medicated, look of stunned astonishment frozen on his face. He was completely mum, except for the occasional mumbled "Not guilty" or "No, Your Honor." No one but investigators and his attorneys had even heard his voice since that brief exchange with a jurist back in the United Kingdom in February 2006.

The photos Neil wanted his lawyer to preserve and send to his parents had already been turned over to prosecutors: pictures that included Neil standing behind his wife and mother-in-law, Priscilla, his arms wrapped protectively around them both, as newborn Lillian rested in her grandmother's arms. Or the picture he took of Rachel sitting in a grassy field with Lillian—looking just like her daddy, save for the smile, which was all her mother's even then. Or the photos of the beloved family dog, Sally, who Neil abandoned, locked in a crate with just a single bowl of water, no food and no way to relieve her bowels, as he fled the country for England. There was the picture of Lillian placed on a little pink puffy seat, confused when her bottom sank into the cushion, a sight that had surely made her parents laugh as they snapped the image. Then there was the photo Rachel had mailed to in-laws so they could see how cute Lilly looked in the pretty pink flowery dress that her grand-mother had sent her from England. There was the one of Neil holding Lilly under a tree; Rachel holding her in front of a flowering bush. Then there was one of Neil, Rachel and Lilly together—taken by a stranger on a beach. In that one, Neil had been fattened by his mother-in-law's homemade food. There was the pic-nic they'd shared, with Neil snapping a shot of Rachel and Lilly spread out on a blanket, and then Rachel tak-ing a picture of Neil with Lilly on the same blanket. Lilly lying on Neil's chest as he sprawled out on the floor of his in-laws' house; Neil hugging Lilly to his chest. Neil holding hands with Rachel; Neil tickling Lilly under her arm pit while whispering in her ear. Lilly's first crawl across the carpet. The three of them together minutes after her birth. Neil and his own par-ents as Yvonne proudly beamed at her granddaughter. Neil hoisting Lilly in front of a lighthouse. Lilly in her skunk costume for Halloween. All of them to-gether at a barbecue in the Matterazzos' back yard.

Love, the happy family, Rachel would write after downloading each one on the family's website. Even after they'd moved, she uploaded pictures to her com-puter, one of the only things not still packed in the boxes that overwhelmed her new home. She wanted so badly for her life to have materialized into that image—of being the perfect wife and mother; for her daughter to grow up with a loving daddy, especially after her own father had died when she was a little girl—that she may have been willing to overlook the subtle signs of Neil's deceptions.

She certainly wouldn't be the first woman to be wooed by a liar, to be seduced by a Prince Charming. Her prince even had a British accent and a loving smile and sexy, secretive job. So even when there started to be signs that not everything was as it seemed—the credit card was frozen, Neil was spending less time in their bed, there were furious customers of his so-called businesses complaining about them online—Rachel held on to her image: *Love, the happy family*.

Even when Neil began to gripe in England that he was being held back, that he would never amount to anything in that country, Rachel persevered, said good-bye to her beloved students, did what was necessary, in her mind's eye, to keep her husband by her side at any cost. *Love, the happy family*. When they'd moved back to the United States, with a brand-new baby no less, and Neil had trouble landing a job, even then, she did not want to believe she had been bamboozled. She was so desperate to be loved that Neil's affections toward her were like crumbs thrown to the starving.

Then, all so briefly, it seemed that everything would be all right. They moved into a house that Neil promised to buy her after just a few months of renting, a brand-new abode in a fancy neighborhood that would be the envy of all her college friends. But Rachel would never even have a chance to unpack. The only thing she was able to set up were the framed photographs of her family, her happy family, hanging them on walls, placing them on shelves, before a bullet was fired into her head, and another rammed through her left breast—only after it had passed through the body of her baby girl—ending her schoolgirl dream of living happily ever after with the man she loved, and who loved her.

Rachel's mother bought into the same lie about Neil, grateful that her daughter had found the happiness that had eluded Priscilla in those long years after her husband Paul had died. Back when her life consisted of nothing more than raising her children and spending her nights alone, tossing and turning in a king-size bed that once held her husband, her lover. Back before she met Joseph Matterazzo, her handsome, hulking hero. Her rock. Who wouldn't want to think that Rachel would not have to go through the loneliness, the pain that Priscilla had gone through in her young adult years? Who wouldn't embrace the quiet, friendly and super-intelligent Brit as a son, especially a man who looked at his wife with such adoration, who played with his baby daughter all the time? Why wouldn't Priscilla want to think that her daughter would have it better than she did in her twenties and thirties? Who wouldn't want to believe that her daughter was loved and extraordinarily happy?

Before Neil Entwistle purportedly stole the .22 from Joseph Matterazzo's gun collection, he was already armed with the ultimate weapon to commit the kind of heinous crime prosecutors believe he pulled off: the trust and love of his victims.

But he certainly did not have the trust, or the love,

of Priscilla Matterazzo anymore. In fact, the loathing she felt for him was also gnawing at her, as damaging to her psyche as her grief, as her humiliation, that he had made such a fool of them all. He poked at Priscilla's painful wound of hatred every time he mentioned having his ashes sprinkled over Rachel and Lilly's grave, making her increasingly determined that she would do everything humanly possible to prevent that from ever happening. She made it clear to every police officer, every prosecutor and even her husband's close friend Joe Flaherty—who was a man of his word—that she wanted them to do whatever it took to keep Neil Entwistle's ashes away from her family. In fact, talking about the sacrilege of his so-called last wish was the only time Priscilla felt any real passion for anything. Her loss had numbed her. The idea that Neil could tell people, not once, but twice, that he wanted to have his rotten, soulless remains in the same cemetery as her daughter and granddaughter sickened her to the point that Priscilla spat out the following words slowly:

"If the bastard kills himself, and I pray God that he does, not a single ash will come near the grave of my daughter and granddaughter. Not a single ash. What do I need to do to make sure that man never comes near their grave? That can't happen. If it does, it will kill me."

Joseph Matterazzo privately said he would stand there with one of his weapons before he would let anyone near the gravesite from Neil Entwistle's camp. Already, the couple was exploring how to obtain a court order to prevent their son-in-law, whose name they couldn't bring to their lips, from being able to come near the grave. Investigators assured Priscilla that she could get a restraining order against Neil Entwistle even in case of his death. Neil had relinquished all rights to be buried with his wife when he signed over Rachel and Lillian's bodies to the care of the Matterazzos with a callous phone call from England more than a year earlier.

After all, Neil had written to Weinstein that he didn't want his body to cause any fanfare. Certainly, "fanfare" would be an understatement if anyone tried to bring his ashes to the Evergreen Cemetery. It was the only place where Priscilla could pray and talk to her daughter in peace.

Besides, as far as Priscilla Matterazzo was concerned, Neil was as good as dead already. She had removed every picture of him from her home, every mention of him in any legal documents pertaining to Rachel's estate. She had seized each and every memento belonging to her daughter and granddaughter from the Hopkinton house and discarded anything left behind by Neil. She would never, ever speak to his parents in England, and prayed each day that they would not show up for his trial. At that time, she wasn't even sure if she was going to go herself.

Let him rot in hell where he belongs.

"If Neil kills himself, or if he is convicted, or even in the unlikelihood that he is acquitted, there is no closure here for Priscilla," Joe Flaherty says every time someone asks him how Rachel's family is holding up. "You hear all the time about closure in these cases, but I don't know if anyone ever finds closure, even if he's found guilty. There might be a little bit of peace that comes when justice is meted out, but they know that Rachel and Lillian are never going to walk back in that door."

Just as Flaherty had predicted when he watched his friend Joe Matterazzo physically restrain Priscilla from toppling over into the grave that held her daughter and granddaughter, she had yet to recover from the shock of it, the betrayal. It is doubtful that she ever will.

The last pictures filed in the photo folder found on Neil's laptop, the ones that he was requesting be sent to his parents in Worksop, were from Lillian's christening. In one of the photographs, Rachel stood in front of Joe Matterazzo, who towered a good foot above her. Neil stood shoulder-to-shoulder with Priscilla. Neil held Lillian, her long, white christening gown flowing down to his knees. Priscilla Matterazzo, in fact, had made the gown herself and Rachel had worn it to her own baptism twenty-seven years earlier. Neil looked as if he would burst with happiness, cuddling his angelic baby girl to his chest, surrounded by his beautiful wife and the American family that had invited them into their tight-knit fold. Behind them was the altar where Lillian Rose Entwistle had just received what Catholics believe was the most important sacrament, the one that guaranteed that a child would go to heaven.

During the ceremony, water was poured over Lillian's head, prompting her to cry out at the chilly surprise. But she was not a cantankerous baby given to wailing jags. After just a few minutes rocking in her daddy's arms, as Rachel, Priscilla and Joe cooed at her and soothed her, Lilly was calm again. Then her parents and grandparents lit a candle on the altar, symbolic of the ever-present light of Christ that would be in Lillian's life. As candles flickered around him, the priest—the same priest who would, just weeks later, hold a funeral Mass for Rachel and Lillian—recited a line from the Sacrament:

"Shine as a light in the world to fight against sin and the Devil."

After the water was poured, purifying her from sin, Lillian Rose was formally baptized as a Catholic. Joseph and Priscilla Matterazzo were viewed by the Church as her godparents, responsible for bringing her up in the unthinkable instance that something would happen to Rachel and Neil. Before the ceremony ended, Neil Entwistle pledged three things out loud in front of God to announce that he was a worthy father to his baby daughter, a proud Catholic capable of bringing up Lillian Rose in the protective fold of the Church: that he repented for his sins; that he turned his life over to Christ; and that he renounced evil.

The people captured smiling in the baby's christening photograph were peaceful that day, knowing that Lilly would now be protected in the palm of God's hand. Priscilla had her hand on the small of Neil's back, her pink blazer accentuating the proud flush of joy that had spread on her cheeks. Rachel had her hands clasped in front of her, a white shawl wrapped around her petite shoulders as she leaned into Neil's girth, ecstatic that her life was just right. Joe Matterazzo stood behind Rachel, one hand tucked in his front pocket, with a wide grin wrinkling the corners of his eyes. Neil pulled Lillian close to his chest with both hands.

As Neil held his baby, smiling, surrounded by the people who had come to love him, not one of them had any idea that he would come to represent the worst kind of evil among them.